D1305812

COMPACT *Research*

Abortion

by Lauri S. Friedman

Current Issues

ReferencePoint
Press™

San Diego, CA

For more information, contact:
ReferencePoint Press, Inc.
PO Box 27779
San Diego, CA 92198
www.ReferencePointPress.com

Picture credits:
Maury Aaseng: 34–37, 51–54, 72–75, 90–92
AP Images: 14, 17

Friedman, Lauri S.
  Abortion / by Lauri S. Friedman.
    p. cm. — (Compact research series)
  ISBN-13: 978-1-60152-047-0 (hardback)
  ISBN-10: 1-60152-047-6 (hardback)
  1. Abortion—Juvenile literature. 2. Abortion—United States—Juvenile literature. I. Title.
  HQ767.F75 2008
  363.460973—dc22
                                                                            2008000341

Contents

Foreword

66 **Where is the knowledge we have lost in information?** 99

—"The Rock," T.S. Eliot.

As modern civilization continues to evolve, its ability to create, store, distribute, and access information expands exponentially. The explosion of information from all media continues to increase at a phenomenal rate. By 2020 some experts predict the worldwide information base will double every 73 days. While access to diverse sources of information and perspectives is paramount to any democratic society, information alone cannot help people gain knowledge and understanding. Information must be organized and presented clearly and succinctly in order to be understood. The challenge in the digital age becomes not the creation of information, but how best to sort, organize, enhance, and present information.

ReferencePoint Press developed the *Compact Research* series with this challenge of the information age in mind. More than any other subject area today, researching current issues can yield vast, diverse, and unqualified information that can be intimidating and overwhelming for even the most advanced and motivated researcher. The *Compact Research* series offers a compact, relevant, intelligent, and conveniently organized collection of information covering a variety of current topics ranging from illegal immigration and methamphetamine to diseases such as anorexia and meningitis.

The series focuses on three types of information: objective single-author narratives, opinion-based primary source quotations, and facts and statistics. The clearly written objective narratives provide context and reliable background information. Primary source quotes are carefully selected and cited, exposing the reader to differing points of view. And facts and statistics sections aid the reader in evaluating perspectives. Presenting these key types of information creates a richer, more balanced learning experience.

For better understanding and convenience, the series enhances information by organizing it into narrower topics and adding design features that make it easy for a reader to identify desired content. For example, in *Compact Research: Illegal Immigration*, a chapter covering the economic impact of illegal immigration has an objective narrative explaining the various ways the economy is impacted, a balanced section of numerous primary source quotes on the topic, followed by facts and full-color illustrations to encourage evaluation of contrasting perspectives.

The ancient Roman philosopher Lucius Annaeus Seneca wrote, "It is quality rather than quantity that matters." More than just a collection of content, the *Compact Research* series is simply committed to creating, finding, organizing, and presenting the most relevant and appropriate amount of information on a current topic in a user-friendly style that invites, intrigues, and fosters understanding.

Abortion
at a Glance

Abortion Rate in the United States

Abortion has been declining in the United States since the 1980s. In the twenty-first century, American women obtain about 1.3 million abortions every year. About 24 percent of all pregnancies end in abortion.

Since *Roe v. Wade*

Since 1973, when abortion became legal in the United States following the Supreme Court's decision in *Roe v. Wade*, more than 46 million abortions have been performed.

Abortion and Parenting

Six in 10 American women who have abortions already have other children and tend to cite the needs of these children as the reason why they cannot have another one.

Abortion Safety Rates

Abortion is considered a safe medical procedure. Less than 0.3 percent of abortion patients experience a complication that requires hospitalization, and a woman is 10 times more likely to die in childbirth than to die from an abortion.

Abortion and Breast Cancer

The National Cancer Institute and American Cancer Society have found no statistically significant link between breast cancer and abortion.

Abortion Access

Eighty-seven percent of Americans live in a county that does not have an abortion clinic. Furthermore, about 25 percent of women seeking an abortion must travel 50 or more miles to the nearest clinic. Between 1996 and 2000, the number of U.S. abortion providers declined by 11 percent.

Gestational Age

Ninety percent of all abortions occur in the first trimester, or when the fetus is 12 weeks or younger.

Rape

Each year, an estimated 13,000 American women have abortions after becoming pregnant as a result of rape and/or incest.

"Partial Birth" Abortion

In 2007 the Supreme Court upheld a ban on "partial birth" abortion, a rarely used late-term abortion procedure that doctors refer to as a dilation and extraction (D&X). For the first time since *Roe v. Wade*, an exception was not made for the life or health of the mother.

Fetal Viability

Thirty-six states prohibit abortion after the point of "fetal viability," or when a fetus is determined able to survive if born prematurely. Exceptions are made in the case the abortion would benefit the health or save the life of the mother.

Fetal Development

A fetus has started to develop eyes, arms, legs, teeth, ears, and a heart by the ninth week of pregnancy. These organs are not fully formed but will continue to develop over the coming weeks and months. Some Americans form their opinion on whether abortion is moral by evaluating to what extent these fetal developments represent life.

Minors and Abortion

Thirty-five states have laws that require women under the age of 18 seeking abortions to notify or obtain permission from their parents for an abortion. All of these states have a "judicial bypass" option that allows the teen to get permission from a judge in the event it is unsafe for her to notify her parents.

Teen Pregnancy and Abortion

Pregnant teenagers account for 19 percent of all abortions.

Waiting Periods

Twenty-four states require a woman seeking an abortion to wait a certain amount of time in between being examined and receiving an abortion. These periods range from 1 hour to 48 hours, with most requiring a 24-hour waiting period.

Mandatory Counseling

Twenty-eight states require women to receive counseling before they have an abortion.

The Abortion Pill

The Food and Drug Administration (FDA) approved a drug called mifepristone in 2000. Since then, 650,000 American women have taken it. Five women have died as a result of a bacterial infection after taking the pill, but no causal link has been made by the federal government.

Overview

Few issues polarize Americans like abortion. It is a highly emotional issue that for decades has had people arguing whether society should allow women to end their unwanted pregnancies. Battles have taken place in courtrooms and clinics, using both pens and bombs. Indeed, abortion is a topic that is an iconoclastic representative of liberty, privacy, and morality issues—and access to it is sure to be debated in America for decades to come. In studying abortion, it is important to understand who in America is having abortions, why they do so, and the implications this has on society and individual liberty.

Who Has Abortions?

American women in all walks of life obtain abortions, but some groups access abortion more than others. For example, the poorer a woman, the more likely she is to have an unwanted pregnancy that ends in abortion. The Guttmacher Institute, a reproduction research group considered authoritative by both antiabortion and abortion rights groups, says that poor women are 4 times more likely to have an abortion than wealthy women, and 57 percent of all women who abort are poor. Race is also a factor in who has abortions—black women are more than 3 times and Latino women are 2½ times as likely to have abortions as are white women. Still, no racial or ethnic group makes up a majority of women who have abortions. Forty-one percent of women who abort are white, 32 percent are black, 20 percent are Hispanic, and 7 percent are of other backgrounds.

> **Women who already have children are in the majority of women who have abortions—6 in 10 women who have abortions are already parents.**

Women who already have children are in the majority of women who have abortions—6 in 10 women who have abortions are already parents. Finally, age and marital status are factors—the majority of abortions (56 percent) are had by women in their twenties, and 67 percent of all women who abort are unwed. Another quality shared by women who abort is that they tend to live in cities—88 percent are classified as urban dwellers.

Why Do Women Choose Abortion?

Why do some women choose to bear children while others choose to abort? And why do some women choose both over the course of their lifetime? Understanding the reasons why women choose to abort certain pregnancies and deliver others is often a matter of understanding why they became unexpectedly pregnant in the first place. For some women, the circumstances surrounding their pregnancy help determine their need for an abortion. If a woman has become pregnant due to rape or incest, for example, she tends to not want to raise a child that is created out of that terrible and traumatic event. Other women unexpectedly conceive during periods in which they have abused alcohol or drugs, and abort out of fear the fetus's health will be compromised.

Finances are another reason women say they choose to end unexpected pregnancies. It is very expensive to raise a child (according to a 2004 report, it costs about $167,000 to raise an American child from birth to age 18, and more if parents help pay for college). For poorer women or women who already have families to support, the financial burden of an additional child is unrealistic or undesirable. In fact, 75 percent of women considering abortions cite economic pressure and finances as a reason.

Finally, women abort unexpected pregnancies due to a plethora of personal reasons. They may feel too young or too old for parenthood. They may be single, or in a relationship not ready for that level of responsibility. They may be married to a partner who does not want children. They may already be parents and feel compelled to devote their time and resources to their already existing children. They may become pregnant during school and believe that a baby will interfere with their education and potential job prospects.

But not all abortions result from unexpected pregnancies. Sometimes, pregnancies end in abortion even when a woman was trying to conceive. In this case, aborted pregnancies are usually due to a health issue in either the baby or mother. Some women develop life-threatening conditions, such as heart problems, as a result of their pregnancy. They must abort to save their own lives (and in many cases must make this decision prior to the point at which the fetus would be able to survive without the mother).

In other cases, health problems in the child cause women to abort. By around the sixteenth week of pregnancy, it can be determined whether a fetus has a health condition that can range from having a disability such as Down syndrome to a life-threatening genetic abnormality such as being born without a face or brain. The women who choose to abort genetically compromised children feel life will be too difficult for both mother and child. These and other reasons are among those regarding why women choose abortion. As one author put it, "The reasons that women have abortions are, in fact, as varied as the women themselves."[1]

Is Abortion a Form of Eugenics?

Increasingly, an interesting facet of the abortion debate is whether it constitutes a form of eugenics. Eugenics is a process by which "undesirable" traits are slowly bred out of the human population. But controversy abounds over what constitutes an undesirable trait and who gets to decide this. The desirability of being short or tall, male or female, blonde or brunette is subjective. Selecting any one of them out of the gene pool is a monumental notion fraught with moral and ethical land mines. Historically, eugenics has been used as a justification for discrimination, human rights violations, and even the murder of whole groups of people. During World War II, for example, the Nazis embarked on a wide-scale killing program to eliminate from the gene pool minorities they considered undesirable, such as Jews, Gypsies, homosexuals, and others.

> **For some women, the circumstances surrounding their pregnancy help determine their need for an abortion.**

Though they constitute a small percent of all abortions, some women choose to abort after learning that their child will be born with a genetic disability or abnormality. The level of attention, care, resources, and emotional strain it would take to raise such a child is a cause to abort, they claim. Said one woman who aborted her baby when it was diagnosed with spina bifida in the womb, "Even if our baby had a remote chance of surviving, it was not a life that we would choose for our child."[2]

But from some perspectives, abortion for this reason constitutes a form of eugenics. Those such as *Washington Post* reporter Patricia E. Bauer see the decision to abort due to genetic imperfection as a type of prenatal discrimination resulting in whole groups of people being eliminated from the human race. Bauer notes that, in particular, parents who learn their unborn baby has Down syndrome are aborting in such high numbers that this group of disabled people is threatened with extinction. "In ancient Greece, babies with disabilities were left out in the elements to die," she explains. "We in America rely on prenatal genetic testing to make our selections in private, but the effect on society is the same. Margaret's [her daughter with Down syndrome] old pediatrician tells me that years ago he used to have a steady stream of patients with Down syndrome. Not anymore. Where did they go, I wonder. On the west side of L.A., they aren't being born anymore."[3] Indeed, about 30 percent of the more than 61,500 Down syndrome fetuses that are conceived each year in the United States end up being aborted. Bauer is appalled that other mothers of Down syndrome kids would think their lives weren't worth living, especially considering that contemporary society has more resources than ever to help people with disabilities live full, happy, productive lives. She views laws that allow women to abort disabled fetuses as inconsistent with laws that protect the rights of people with disabilities once they are born.

A Parent's Difficult Decision

Yet others argue that although difficult and unpleasant, it remains important for women to have the right to abort a baby that tests positive for genetic diseases and abnormalities. In the case of one woman, her fetus was diagnosed with an abnormality that caused it to develop without a face. Giving birth to this doomed baby would have been emotionally scarring, and also threaten her future fertility. In other cases, a woman may retain the right to abort genetically imperfect fetuses because it remains her right to decide not only whether she wants to have a baby but also what kind of impact that child will have on her life. Explains one woman who chose to abort a fetus that would have been born with a severe disability: "I made a choice based on my own and my family's needs and limitations. I did not want to raise a genetically compromised child. I did not want my children to have to contend with the massive diversion of parental attention and the consequences of being compelled to care for their brother after I died."[4]

Of course, opinions over whether genetically imperfect fetuses should be born are subjective and wide-ranging. Another mother, Brenda Hanson, gave birth to her genetically compromised daughter Sarah. Despite the fact that Sarah has Down syndrome, leukemia, and Moyamoya syndrome (which causes strokes), and is a quadriplegic who will require diapers and a feeding tube for the rest of her life, her mother has "never, ever, ever thought of Sarah as an 'error.' . . . Sarah's Down syndrome and other medical struggles have meaningful purpose that I, as a parent, am responsible for helping her discover and then sharing with the world."[5] Differing

> " Some see the decision to abort due to genetic imperfection as a type of prenatal discrimination resulting in whole groups of people being eliminated from the human race. "

This protest took place in Sioux Falls, South Dakota, in 2006. South Dakota only has one abortion clinic, and there isn't one doctor in the entire state that will perform abortions. Doctors from neighboring Minnesota fly in to perform scheduled abortions.

perspectives on the responsibility of parents explain why abortion is continually a passionately debated topic.

Using Abortion to Eliminate Women

Another example of how prenatal testing is making it possible for abortion to be used eugenically comes from nations such as China and India, where increasing numbers of female fetuses are being aborted. These countries have cultures in which it is auspicious to give birth to boys, and they are also suffering from a population boom. China is so crowded, in fact, that parents there are only allowed to have one child. To ensure it is a boy, millions of Chinese are aborting female fetuses each year. It is estimated that 130 Chinese boys are now born for every 100 girls—naturally, there should be about 104 Chinese boys born for every 100 girls. Douglas A. Sylva of the Catholic Family and Human Rights Institute points out that such a grave gender imbalance could have enormous social, demographic, geopolitical, and even military consequences. "Nobody knows what will happen to a society in which 40 million men cannot find wives," he writes, "but already, there are reports of widespread rapes, forced marriages, and human trafficking. In 10 years time, when the problem is more acute, the Chinese government might even find it necessary to send its excess men on a military 'adventure' of some kind, in order to mitigate the social instability at home."[6]

> **The legalization of abortion standardized the procedure, moving it from dirty, dangerous sites such as alleys, cars, and hotel rooms to sterile, safe hospitals and clinics.**

China is not the only nation practicing sex-selective abortion. El Salvador, Egypt, Libya, Luxembourg, and India are among the nations witnessing an influx of blue bassinets rather than pink in their hospital wards. The implications of sex-selective abortion in these countries is not just a demographic matter, but an ironic one. Abortion has for decades been an integral part of the women's liberation movement due to the way in which it gives women control over their fertility. So one can, writes Sylva, "imagine the shock and shame when it became obvious that many of these newly-liberated women have been using their liberty to abort their own unborn girls."[7] The full effects of sex-selective abortion remain to be seen, but abortion advocates say that this tragic use of abortion should not be used as an excuse to take away other women's right to legal and safe abortion.

How Safe Is Abortion?

Because abortion is a medical procedure, there is a risk of injury. Among the complications that can occur during an abortion are excessive bleeding, perforation of the uterus, severe infection, future infertility, and even death. However, such complications are exceedingly rare in the post-*Roe* world; the legalization of abortion standardized the procedure, moving it from dirty, dangerous sites such as alleys, cars, and hotel rooms to sterile, safe hospitals and clinics. The Guttmacher Institute calls abortion "one of the safest surgical procedures for women in the United States."[8] It reports that less than 0.3 percent of women experience an abortion-related complication and that the risk of death associated with abortion is about one-tenth to one-twelfth the risk of childbirth.

Despite its overall safety, however, deaths from abortion do still occur. According to the Centers for Disease Control and Prevention, there have been between 4 and 12 deaths from legal or illegal abortion every year for the past 10 years. The risk of death associated with abortion increases with the length of pregnancy. Women have just a 1 in 1 million chance of dying from an abortion performed before the ninth week of pregnancy. That risk increases to 1 in 29,000 if the abortion is performed at 16–20 weeks, and 1 in 11,000 at 21 or more weeks. Clearly, the longer a woman waits to have an abortion, the more she risks her health.

> Differing perspectives on the responsibility of parents explain why abortion is continually a passionately debated topic.

A point of debate when people discuss the safety of abortion is whether the procedure comes with a higher risk of developing breast cancer. Pro-life groups charge that women who undergo abortions are at a higher risk for breast cancer as a result of abrupt hormonal changes in the no-longer-pregnant woman. While some university studies have shown a mild link, exhaustive studies undertaken by the National Cancer Institute, the American Cancer Society, and the British government have found no statistically significant link between abortion and breast or any other type of cancer. Despite the lack of evidence for an abortion–breast cancer link, states such as Texas, Kansas, and Minnesota require abortion

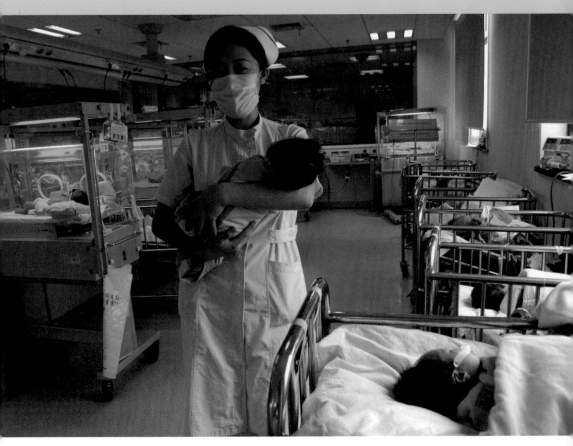

In China increasing numbers of female fetuses are being aborted. Countries such as China and India have cultures in which it is auspicious to give birth to boys, and they are also suffering from a population boom. China is so crowded, in fact, that parents there are only allowed to have one child. To ensure it is a boy, millions of Chinese are aborting female fetuses or abandoning baby girls each year. This Chinese orphanage is full of baby girls.

providers to inform women about the risk prior to the procedure. For some, such as policy analyst Diana Dukhanova, this is an unfair bogeyman tactic used to scare women out of having abortions and is in the same spirit of how authorities of the past falsely warned teenagers that masturbating would cause hair to grown on their palms: "In its shameless use of bad science to discourage the 'sin' that comes from 'bad' sexuality," she writes, "the Abortion-Breast Cancer link is the 'hairy palm' of the Right-to-Life movement."[9]

Whether experiencing an abortion makes a woman prone to psychological disorders and depression is also a matter of debate. Pro-life groups have repeatedly warned about negative psychological effects that can occur after abortion, including depression, anxiety, sexual inhibition, flashbacks, and a tendency for substance abuse—symptoms that together make up a condition they call post-abortion syndrome (PAS). Some studies have confirmed the existence of PAS. For example, a 2006 study published in the *Journal of Child Psychiatry and Psychology* studied more than 1,200 women over 30 years. It found that those who had an abortion were more likely to experience anxiety, depression, substance abuse, and suicidal tendencies. For this reason, one author has described the psychological consequences of abortion in the following way: "Far from being a victimless crime, abortion kills an innocent passenger and maims the unknowing driver."[10]

> **Exhaustive studies undertaken by the National Cancer Institute, the American Cancer Society, and the British government have found no statistically significant link between abortion and breast or any other type of cancer.**

Yet others dispute the severity and even the existence of post-abortion syndrome. The American Psychiatric Association, for example, does not recognize PAS as a legitimate condition. According to Planned Parenthood, about 20 percent of women experience only mild and temporary depression after an abortion, and severe depression occurs in less than 0.02 percent of patients. Instead, the majority of women report feeling relief after an abortion. Concluded Brenda Major, author of a University of California–Santa Barbara study that found the psychological effects of abortion to be rare, mild, and overstated: "Most women were satisfied with their decision, and believed that they had benefited more than they had been harmed."[11]

The Future of Abortion Access

A changing political climate, the advent of genetic technologies, and a host of other complex variables make the future of abortion rights uncertain in the United States. Yet one very simple factor looming over the future of abortion is the declining number of abortion providers. Between 1996 and 2000, the number of U.S. abortion providers declined by 11 percent, and it is expected that the number of doctors trained in the procedure will continue to decline over the next 10–20 years. Indeed, 57 percent of all abortion doctors are 50 years old or older, and will soon be due to retire. Furthermore, their replacements are not being trained, as abortions tend to take place in clinics rather than hospitals, where most medical students learn surgical techniques. If medical students are not taught to perform abortions in hospitals, it is unlikely many of them will choose to specialize in the procedure.

And even if medical students intern in abortion clinics, those too are on the decline. In 2008, there were abortion clinics in just 13 percent of American counties. This means that 87 percent of the nation's population must travel out of county, and sometimes out of state, to access abortion services. Some states have reduced their abortion facilities so drastically that they have just one clinic in the whole state, as is the case in South Dakota. In fact, abortion is so taboo in that state that no South Dakota physician will perform them—doctors fly in from neighboring Minnesota to help South Dakota women end their unwanted pregnancies. On the other hand, the declining number of abortion clinics could be mitigated by the increase in women who choose to end their unwanted pregnancies using the abortion pill, a nonsurgical abortion method. To use the abortion pill, women need only have it prescribed to them by a doctor, and thus could in the future rely less on clinics and more on the prescription pad to access their right to choose.

> " The majority of women report feeling relief after an abortion. "

Abortion is one of the most emotional, personal, and fiercely debated issues in contemporary American society. Each new decade witnesses changing opinions on abortion, and thus laws that reflect that. But whether abortion rights are expanded or restricted, curbed or enhanced, people are likely to continue to debate its morality and legality with fervor and conviction for years to come.

Is Abortion Immoral?

66 I kept seeing the picture of that tiny, ten-week-old embryo and I said to myself, "That's a baby!" I finally understood the truth: *That's a baby!* 99

—Norma McCorvey, "Jane Roe" of the *Roe v. Wade* court case that legalized abortion.

66 By whatever rationale you use, ending a pregnancy 12 weeks into gestation is incalculably more moral than bringing an unwanted child into this world. 99

—Caitlin Moran, columnist for the *Times* of London.

Though abortion has been legal since 1973, whether the procedure is moral is an ongoing matter of debate that produces a wide variety of perspectives. To a slim percentage of Americans, abortion is always immoral (about 16 percent of the American public, according to a 2006 AP-Ipsos poll) or always moral (about 19 percent). To the majority, however, the details of a pregnancy determine whether abortion is a moral choice. For example, many Americans agree it is moral to obtain an abortion if one has become pregnant due to rape, or if a pregnancy threatens a mother's health. Others might deem it moral for a young teenager with her whole life in front of her to abort, but would judge as immoral the decision of a wealthy, married 35-year-old to abort. A person's opinion on whether abortion is moral usually depends on religious, spiritual, or humanitarian convictions that inform his or her opinion about life's origins, human rights, and equality.

The question of when life begins is central to the issue of whether abortion is moral. Depending on the answer, abortion is viewed as everything from a simple medical procedure, to the ending of potential life, to outright murder.

Antiabortionists believe that life begins at conception, and abortion is immoral because it is equivalent to murder. There is perhaps no more powerful voice in the antiabortion camp on this matter than Norma McCorvey, who was the famous "Jane Roe" of the 1973 *Roe v. Wade* case in which abortion became legal. Following the case, McCorvey became vehemently antiabortion on the grounds that she viewed it as killing. "I had to face up to the awful reality that abortion was not about 'products of conception' or 'missed periods,'" she said. "It was about children being killed in their mothers' wombs."[12] Perhaps this is why 45 percent of American Catholics and Protestants think abortion should be illegal—because they believe that abortion is nothing short of the taking of a life. Indeed, the bond a woman can form with her unborn child—in the weeks, and days, even, of becoming pregnant—is considered to be one of the most powerful she will ever know. As one woman who lost her pregnancy while considering abortion put it, "The feeling of attachment to the unborn child is powerful. . . . It is important to realize that the attachment is not 'small' because the child is still small."[13]

Yet many others view pregnancy as the biological beginnings of life rather than fully developed life. As a result, they deem abortion to be a moral response to a difficult problem. In the earliest stages of pregnancy, when the majority of abortions occur, a fertilized egg is biologically not much more than a rapidly dividing group of cells. Over the weeks it develops in greater detail, but in the first trimester (when the overwhelming majority of abortions occur) it does not have any of the qualities that are normally assigned to life—such as the capacity to think, feel, or experience. Because of this, a distinction is often made between the biological reality of an early fetus and the life of a fully developed older fetus or infant. As one theology professor has put it, "To claim that a fertilized egg within days of conception is a human person is a totally platonic view of the human person. It means there is a human soul fully

> **The question of when life begins is central to the issue of whether abortion is moral.**

present in a tiny speck of germ plasma."[14] From this perspective, aborting an undeveloped fetus is moral—and especially if it prevents a life of suffering for either the mother or the potential baby. One woman who aborted a fetus stricken with spina bifida explained it in the following way: "Even if our baby had a remote chance of surviving, it was not a life that we would choose for our child."[15]

> **The bond a woman can form with her unborn child—in the weeks, and days, even, of becoming pregnant—is considered to be one of the most powerful she will ever know.**

Many Americans find common ground in the idea that a fertilized egg or weeks-old fetus is not a full human, yet it also is not *nothing*. Rather, they view it as "a potential life that is in process of actualization."[16] Deciding whether it is moral to end or continue that potential life is intensely personal, and a dilemma for which there is not necessarily one wrong or right answer. Many women choose to abort even when they acknowledge their pregnancy is more to them than a biological matter. Says Ayelet Waldman, who aborted her child because it had a life-threatening genetic abnormality, "This was, for me, a baby, not a 'clump of cells,' as an older woman, steeped in the arcane language of the early feminist movement, called him. He was my baby, and I chose to end his life."[17] Waldman is a good example of how an opinion about when life begins does not necessarily determine how a woman will react when faced with an unwanted pregnancy—she chose to abort despite her belief that her fetus was a baby, not just biology.

While the Supreme Court has not specifically ruled on the question, its opinion on when life begins has informed its verdicts on abortion. In the landmark 1973 case *Roe v. Wade*, which legalized abortion, the Court used the concept of "fetal viability"—the point at which a fetus has the capacity to survive outside the womb—to rule on placing legal limits on abortion. Although each fetus develops on a unique timeframe, each is considered viable when critical organs, such as the lungs and kidneys, can sustain him or her outside the womb, which occurs around 24 weeks of age. After this point, the fetus gains substantial autonomy and is considered by legal standards to be capable of living and thus is given more rights under the law. The issue of fetal viability is therefore a barometer for decisions on whether to legalize abortion, and at what point in time.

The Role of Technology in Determining When Life Begins

In the twenty-first century, technology is pushing the limits on fetal viability, further obscuring the issue of when life begins. When abortion became legal in 1973, prenatal diagnostic tools such as ultrasound and amniocentesis—tests that provide detailed information and visual pictures of the fetus in the womb—were just beginning to be developed. Thirty-five years later, however, not only can parents see images of their baby as young as four and a half weeks old, but a whole field of fetal medicine has emerged that is devoted to treating babies in utero (in the womb).

Doctors are now able to determine the sex of the baby, diagnose fetal abnormalities, screen for chromosomal problems, and even perform intrauterine (in-womb) surgery. Other technologies allow babies to be born so prematurely that they can survive at the same age as other fetuses that are considered for abortion. To those who oppose abortion, these technologies make it clearer than ever that a fetus is a baby that has the potential—and right—to live. As one such technological advance caused one editor to comment, "For the first time [in February 2007], a baby born at 22 weeks is thriving. Perhaps her example will cause some people to . . . ask why a 22-week-old can be a patient in one hospital room and a 'terminated pregnancy' in another."[18]

> " In the early weeks of pregnancy a fertilized egg develops in greater detail, but does not have any of the qualities that are normally assigned to life—such as the capacity to think, feel, or experience. "

Pro-life advocates point out that these technologies have lowered the bar of when a fetus is considered a baby. Some pro-life pregnancy centers offer women a free ultrasound and the chance to connect with their unborn child. In one clinic, nurse Joyce Wilson says that in 2 months, 5 women decided to keep their babies after seeing their image on an ultrasound. "They connected, they bonded," said Wilson. "You could just see it. One girl got off the table and said, 'That's my baby.'"[19] According to one survey of pregnancy clinic practitioners, as many as 50 percent of pregnant women decide not to abort after seeing a sonogram of their fetus. Indeed, neonatal technology is powerfully underscoring the anti-abortion movement's entire premise: that the unborn are people waiting to happen.

Respecting Those Who Are Already Alive

But is allowing the unborn a chance at life always the right thing to do? Not if it conflicts with the rights, desires, and health of the already living say many in the pro-choice camp. Indeed, the rights of the living have been legally deemed more valid than the rights of a fetus in two main ways: how those rights affect a pregnant woman and how they affect her other children.

Roe v. Wade decreed that the right of a woman to choose her own destiny trumps the right of a fetus to potential life. In first trimester pregnancies, this means that a woman—for whatever reason—has the right to end her pregnancy if she thinks it will interfere with her education, job prospects, health, living situation, or any other aspect of her life. If a woman becomes pregnant, either accidentally or by force, it is her right to choose that her future not be dictated by that event. Coral Lopez is one woman whose access to abortion allowed her to keep the future she always dreamed for herself. Because she was able to have an abortion when she got pregnant as a teenager, "I became the first person in my family to graduate high school, the first person to graduate from college." In this way, Lopez says abortion "saved *my* life."[20]

> **Many Americans find common ground in the idea that a fertilized egg or weeks-old fetus is not a full human, yet it also is not *nothing*.**

Another way in which the rights of the living make abortion a moral choice for supporters is when already-living children are taken into account. Interestingly, a majority of American women who have abortions are already mothers. According to a 2006 report by the Guttmacher Institute, 6 in 10—about 61 percent—of women who have abortions already have other children. They choose to abort their pregnancy precisely because they believe it will interfere with their ability to adequately parent their other offspring. They get abortions not because they don't want to become parents, but because they want to preserve the quality of life of their already existing children. Another child would add financial and emotional burdens to already strapped homes and reduce the resources and attention devoted to already-living children. One mother, Caitlin Moran, described her choice to end her third pregnancy in the following way: "I knew I would see my existing two daughters less, my husband less, my career would be hamstrung and, most importantly of all, I was just too *tired* to do it all again."[21] In fact, Moran believes her abortion was "one of the ultimate acts of good mothering" because it put the needs of her existing children first.

Rosemary Radford Ruether, a theology professor, is another person who views abortion as a moral act when it will improve a woman's ability to provide for her existing children. Ruether says denying a woman access to abortion "is an example of absolutizing the value of the life of the unborn and disregarding the value of the lives of the born." From this perspective, abortion is the moral choice if having another child would limit a mother's ability to be a good parent to her already existing children. Says Ruether, "This does not mean there are no values to be defended in relation to the unborn, but these must be appropriately balanced in relation to the enormous threats to the lives of the born."[22]

Does the Fetus Feel Pain?

Whether a fetus experiences pain is another question raised when one grapples with the morality of abortion. Of course, the idea of a developing baby experiencing the pain of dying before it has even been born is disturbing to many people. One such person is Dr. Hanes Swingle, a physician who became pro-life after witnessing abortions in which he remembers seeing "the aborted fetus moving its legs and gasping" in pain as it was removed from the uterus.[23] The issue of fetal pain is so important that some states, including Arkansas, Minnesota, and Georgia, require doctors to tell women seeking abortions that 20-week-old fetuses can feel pain during an abortion, and to offer fetal anesthesia to ease this pain. California, Kentucky, Montana, New York, Oregon, Virginia, and the federal government have all considered similar legislation.

> **The issue of fetal viability is a barometer for decisions on whether to legalize abortion, and at what point in time.**

But according to a 2005 report published by University of California–San Francisco researchers, it is unlikely that aborted fetuses feel pain during the procedure. The report analyzed more than 20 other studies that had studied fetal pain and all came to this conclusion. The researchers found that fetuses do not develop the nerve pathways responsible for detecting pain until they are at least 28 weeks old. Fetuses do develop pain receptors as early as 8 weeks old. However, the thalamus, the part of the brain that detects pain from the pain receptors (thus making pain possible to experience), does not develop for another 20 weeks. Since only 1.4 percent of abortions are performed at or after 21 weeks of age, and even fewer are performed after that (due to laws in many states that ban abortion after fetal viability), it is highly unlikely that a fetus will experience pain during abortion.

The researchers explained that some fetuses, such as the one witnessed by Dr. Swingle, appear to experience pain but in reality are responding to reflexes caused by the spinal chord that have nothing to do with pain. Concluded the researchers: "fetal perception of pain is unlikely before the third trimester [which begins at 25 weeks]."[24] The group Catholics for a Free Choice agrees, saying, "It is possible but not probable that fetuses in the range of 20–26 weeks experience pain."[25] With this in mind, researchers at the Guttmacher Institute and elsewhere have expressed concern over laws in some states that encourage women to elect to receive fetal anesthesia during an abortion because it increases a woman's risk of death, and is unnecessary to control pain in a fetus that cannot feel it.

Weighing in on the morality of abortion is an intensely personal matter to which there is no universal answer. Opinions on the morality of abortion are informed by a person's understanding of complex philosophical matters, such as when life begins and the rights of the living. As Swingle put it, "I now realize the difference between a fetus and a premature infant is a social distinction, not a biological one. If it is wanted, it is a baby; if not wanted, it is a fetus."[26] Under the law, that distinction remains possible to make. Determining the morality of abortion is a complicated and confusing matter, but one integrally tied to its legality and prevalence.

Is Abortion Immoral?

❝A lot of times people say that women who have abortions have selfish reasons. No—it was an act of love.❞

—Coral Lopez, interviewed in Ziba Kashef, "Her Body, Her Choice?" *Colorlines*, Winter 2005.

Lopez is a Los Angeles resident whose ability to abort her unwanted pregnancies allowed her to escape a life of poverty.

❝Ultrasound images confront the parents with the irrevocable reality of the humanity of their own developing child. And this helps them instantly realize what was probably hidden in their hearts and minds: taking innocent life is not an option.❞

—Ann V. Shibler, "Saving Babies, One at a Time," *New American*, August 20, 2007.

Shibler is a writer whose articles opposing abortion and euthanasia have appeared in the *New American* magazine.

Bracketed quotes indicate conflicting positions.

* Editor's Note: While the definition of a primary source can be narrowly or broadly defined, for the purposes of Compact Research, a primary source consists of: 1) results of original research presented by an organization or researcher; 2) eyewitness accounts of events, personal experience, or work experience; 3) first-person editorials offering pundits' opinions; 4) government officials presenting political plans and/or policies; 5) representatives of organizations presenting testimony or policy.

66 A return to the moral base upon which this nation was built has to include turning away from abortion. Our nation's Founding Fathers would be horrified at what has happened. 99

—John F. McManus, "Abortion's Effect on America," *New American*, January 23, 2006.

McManus is the president of the John Birch Society, a group dedicated to preserving family values and American freedom.

66 Because pain perception probably does not function before the third trimester, discussions of fetal pain for abortions performed before the end of the second trimester should be noncompulsory. Fetal anesthesia or analgesia should not be recommended or routinely offered for abortion because current experimental techniques provide unknown fetal benefit and may increase risks for the woman. 99

—Susan J. Lee et al., "Fetal Pain: A Systematic Multidisciplinary Review of the Evidence," *Journal of the American Medical Association*, vol. 294, no. 8, August 24–31, 2005.

Lee, Ralston, Drey, Partridge, and Rosen are researchers at the University of California–San Francisco. Their review of available evidence on fetal pain led them to conclude that fetuses do not feel pain until 28 weeks and that women should not elect fetal anesthesia during abortions because it needlessly risks their health.

66 It is possible but not probable that fetuses in the range of 20–26 weeks experience pain, and that even that possibility should lead us to act with caution and aim to diminish or eliminate possible fetal pain during abortion. . . . Fetal anesthesia should be available if, after being informed of the possibility that fetuses feel pain, women choose it. 99

—Catholics for a Free Choice, "Respecting Women's Rights and Fetal Value: Reflections on the Question of Fetal Anesthesia," *Conscience*, Autumn 2005.

Catholics for a Free Choice was founded in 1973 by Catholics who believe that the Catholic tradition should support a woman's right to access safe and legal abortion.

❝No matter where we stand on the spectrum of belief, we ought to cherish the rights of everyone. This is a fundamental principle on which the whole country and the Constitution rely.❞

—Faye Wattleton, interviewed in Akiba Solomon, "The Battle for Reproductive Rights," *Essence*, May 2006.

Wattleton is president of the Center for the Advancement of Women and former president of Planned Parenthood.

❝The Church's opposition to abortion is clear and unconditional. According to the Catechism of the Catholic Church, 'since the first century the church has affirmed the moral evil of every procured abortion. This teaching has not changed and remains unchangeable.❞

—James D. Davidson, "What Catholics Believe About Abortion and the Death Penalty," *National Catholic Reporter*, September 30, 2005.

Davidson is a professor of sociology at Purdue University. His written works include *Catholicism in Motion, Lay Ministers and Their Spiritual Practices*, and *The Search for Common Ground*. He is the president of the Association for the Sociology of Religion.

❝I do not believe that there is a 'human person' present from the first moment of conception, nor do I believe that the Catholic tradition actually teaches this or follows this in its pastoral practice, as is evident from its refusal to baptize even late-term miscarriages.❞

—Rosemary Radford Ruether, "'Consistent Life Ethic' Is Inconsistent," *National Catholic Reporter*, November 17, 2006.

Ruether is a professor of feminist theology at the Graduate Theological Union in Berkeley, California.

"We who were born in the 34 years since *Roe v. Wade* have grown up in a society that does not value human life, that places more importance on ease and convenience than on accountability and responsibility."

—*National Right to Life News*, "The Missing: The Real Impact of Abortion on American Society," January 2007.

National Right to Life News is a publication of National Right to Life, an organization that opposes abortion on the grounds that it is murder.

"As a species, we've fairly comprehensively demonstrated that we don't believe in the sanctity of life. I don't understand why pregnant women—women trying to make rational decisions about their futures—should be subject to more pressure about preserving life than, say, [political leaders who start wars such as Russian president] Vladimir Putin."

—Caitlin Moran, "Abortion: Why It's the Ultimate Motherly Act," *Times* (London), April 13, 2007.

Moran is the mother of two who chose to abort her third pregnancy because an additional child would reduce her family's quality of life.

"Who asks muggers if they *feel* guilty? The act of mugging is wrong in itself. And so is abortion, whether or not women feel it to be so."

—Stan Guthrie, "Don't Cede the High Ground," *Christianity Today*, May 2007.

Guthrie is a writer who contributes regularly to the Foolish Things column in *Christianity Today* magazine.

"The morality of abortion cannot be resolved in the abstract. Each individual abortion takes place within its own complex set of circumstances. To understand abortion, we need to understand its place in women's lives."

—Ann Furedi, "Some Messages Can't Be Massaged, *Conscience*, Winter 2006–2007.

Furedi is the chief executive of the British Pregnancy Advisory Service (BPAS), the United Kingdom's largest independent abortion provider.

"Something happened to make [me] choose life and choose it firmly and reject death. I think it was [my] conscience that intervened or, if you prefer, the basic human instinct that favors life over death. Of, if you are a Christian, as I am, it was God."

—Fred Barnes, "Choosing Life: How Pro-Lifers Become Pro-Lifers," *Weekly Standard*, September 1, 2006.

Barnes is the executive editor of the *Weekly Standard*.

"The reality [is] that, for many women, an abortion is necessary if they're to cope, financially and emotionally, with their existing children."

Kira Cochrane, "'Abortion on Demand' Is a Myth," *New Statesman*, April 23, 2007.

Cochrane is women's editor of the *Guardian*, a British newspaper.

Is Abortion Immoral?

- According to the Guttmacher Institute, in the United States women who have abortions are:
  - in their 20s **(56 percent)**
  - already parents **(61 percent)**
  - unmarried **(67 percent)**
  - poor **(57 percent)**
  - urban dwellers **(88 percent)**
  - religious **(78 percent)**

- Nearly **50 percent** of pregnancies among American women are unintended, 4 in 10 of these are terminated by abortion.

- At current rates, **35 percent** of American women will have at least one abortion by the age of 45.

- Black women are more than **three times** and Latino women are **two and a half times** as likely to have abortions as white women.

- **Forty-three percent** of women having abortions report being Protestant; **27 percent** are Catholic.

- In the United Kingdom, **47 percent** of all women who have an abortion already have at least one child.

Poverty and Unplanned Pregnancy

Poor women are 4 times as likely to have an unplanned pregnancy, 3 times as likely to have an abortion, and 5 times as likely to have an unplanned birth than wealthier women.

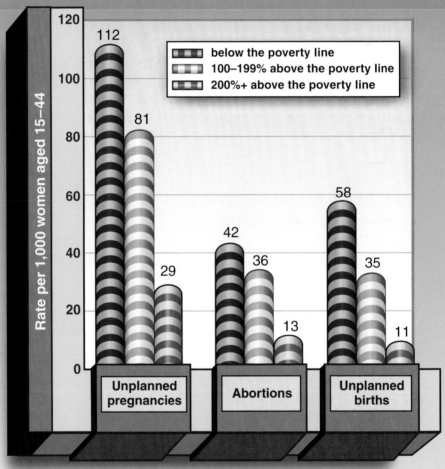

Legend:
- below the poverty line
- 100–199% above the poverty line
- 200%+ above the poverty line

Rate per 1,000 women aged 15–44

Unplanned pregnancies: 112, 81, 29
Abortions: 42, 36, 13
Unplanned births: 58, 35, 11

Source: Rachel Benson Gold, "Rekindling Efforts to Prevent Unplanned Pregnancy: A Matter of 'Equity and Common Sense,'" *Guttmacher Policy Review*, vol. 9, no. 3, 2006.

Reasons for Abortion

In a 2004 study, researchers interviewed more than 1,000 women about their reasons for having an abortion. The women often gave more than one explanation for their decision, but all fell under at least one of the following.

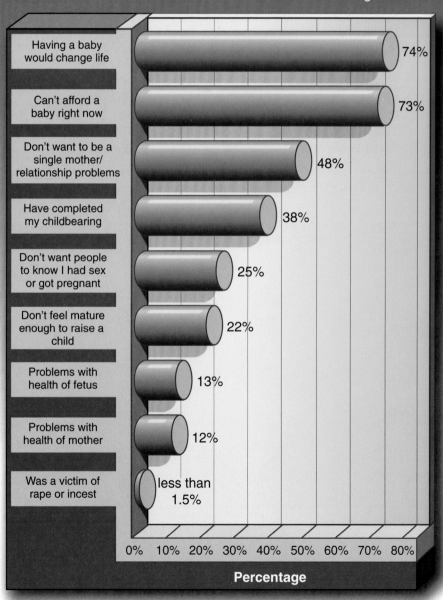

Having a baby would change life	74%
Can't afford a baby right now	73%
Don't want to be a single mother/ relationship problems	48%
Have completed my childbearing	38%
Don't want people to know I had sex or got pregnant	25%
Don't feel mature enough to raise a child	22%
Problems with health of fetus	13%
Problems with health of mother	12%
Was a victim of rape or incest	less than 1.5%

0% 10% 20% 30% 40% 50% 60% 70% 80%

Percentage

Source: Nancy Gibbs, "1 Woman at a Time," *Time*, February 26, 2007.

Increasing Numbers of Pregnancy Crisis Centers

In the United States, hundreds of "pregnancy crisis centers" have sprung up. The mission of these centers is to persuade women considering abortion to change their minds. They do so through biased counseling, by showing women sonogram pictures of their fetus, and telling them that abortion could leave them sterile, mentally ill, or worse. Though their techniques are controversial, such centers now outnumber abortion providers in the United States. There are 2,300 pregnancy crisis centers and 1,819 abortion providers in the country. Two companies, Care Net and Heartbeat International, manage about 75 percent of the centers.

Pregnancy crisis centers managed by Care Net and Heartbeat International

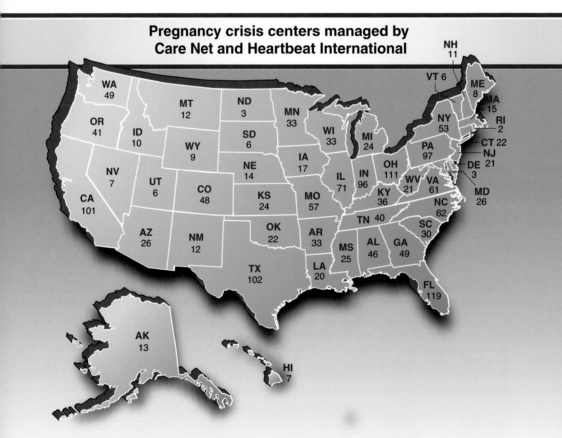

WA 49
OR 41
ID 10
MT 12
ND 3
MN 33
WI 33
MI 24
NH 11
VT 6
ME 8
MA 15
NY 53
RI 2
CT 22
NJ 21
PA 97
DE 3
NV 7
UT 6
WY 9
SD 6
NE 14
IA 17
IL 71
IN 96
OH 111
WV 21
VA 61
MD 26
CA 101
CO 48
KS 24
MO 57
KY 36
NC 62
TN 40
SC 30
AZ 26
NM 12
OK 22
AR 33
MS 25
AL 46
GA 49
TX 102
LA 20
FL 119
AK 13
HI 7

Sources: Guttmacher Institute, Perspectives on Sexual and Reproductive Health, Care Net, Heartbeat International, and National Abortion Federation, 2007.

The Development of Life

A fetus has started to develop eyes, arms, legs, teeth, ears, and a heart by the ninth week of pregnancy. These organs are not fully formed, but will continue to develop over the coming weeks and months. Some Americans form their opinion on whether abortion is moral by evaluating to what extent these fetal developments represent life.

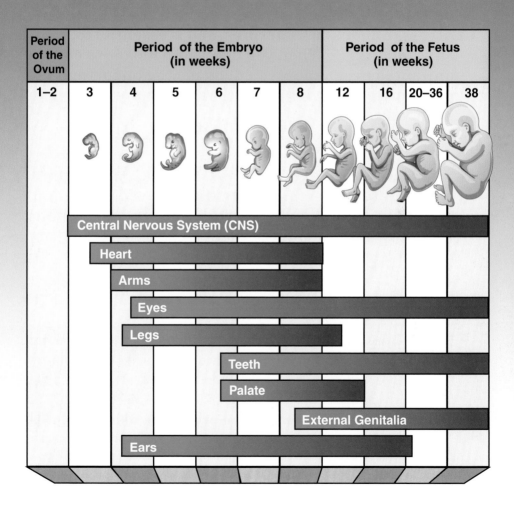

Period of the Ovum	Period of the Embryo (in weeks)						Period of the Fetus (in weeks)			
1–2	3	4	5	6	7	8	12	16	20–36	38

Central Nervous System (CNS)

Heart

Arms

Eyes

Legs

Teeth

Palate

External Genitalia

Ears

Source: National Organization on Fetal Alcohol Syndrome.

Should Abortion Be Legal?

66 Access to abortion underpins, and is essential to, women's equality. . . . When you deny me a means to end my unwanted pregnancy, you deny me the opportunity to participate in society in the way that my brother or husband can.99

—Ann Furedi, chief executive of British Pregnancy Advisory Service (BPAS).

66 It is because I still believe so strongly in the right of a woman to protect her body that I now oppose abortion. That right must begin when her body begins, and it must be hers no matter where she lives—even if she lives in her mother's womb.99

—Frederica Mathewes-Green, pro-life speaker and author.

The discussion over the legality of abortion centers on the idea of personal privacy. This is because when the Supreme Court ruled to legalize abortion in 1973 in the landmark case *Roe v. Wade*, it did so based on the idea that it is a violation of a woman's right to privacy for the government to tell her what she can and can't do with her body.

A Matter of Privacy

A woman's right to access abortion services was declared legal as part of the right to privacy that is guaranteed to all Americans by the Fourteenth Amendment. As Supreme Court justice Potter Stewart wrote in the majority opinion in *Roe v. Wade*, "freedom of personal choice in matters of marriage and family life is one of the liberties protected" under the Constitution.[27] Therefore, the Court struck down existing state laws against abortion on the grounds that they "violate the Due Process Clause of the Fourteenth Amendment, which protects against state action the right to privacy, including a woman's qualified right to terminate her pregnancy."[28]

Interestingly, in making this ruling, the Court acknowledged that its job was not to determine whether abortion is moral or when life begins. Wrote Supreme Court justice Harold M. Blackmun, "We need not resolve the difficult question of when life begins. When those trained in the respective disciplines of medicine, philosophy, and theology are unable to arrive at any consensus, the judiciary, at this point in the development of man's knowledge, is not in a position to speculate as to the answer."[29] The Court was clear that its only job was to determine whether a woman has a right to have an abortion—and it determined that she does, under the Fourteenth Amendment.

> **The Court acknowledged that its job was not to determine whether abortion is moral or when life begins.**

Since the landmark ruling, antiabortionists have opposed the suggestion that abortion is a private matter, arguing pregnancy is not an issue that solely concerns a woman and her body. From some perspectives, life begins at the moment of conception, and thus a pregnant woman carries within her a life that is intimately connected, but not limited, to her domain. Others invoke the rights of fathers, who had just as much a hand in creating a fetus as a mother, yet under this ruling retain no rights to it during gestation. Finally, some believe that unborn babies belong to the entire community, and ultimately, to God.

But under the U.S. Constitution, because a fetus is not yet a legal person, it cannot enjoy the same rights as the living—and thus is the property of the woman in which it resides and is subject to her decisions. Since *Roe v. Wade*, the U.S. Supreme Court has given more than 20 major rulings regarding abortion. While some of these have placed restrictions on abortion—such as banning a late-term abortion procedure or allowing states to require that minors get parental permission to get an abortion—the Court has protected what was established in 1973: that a woman has a legal right to access abortion services.

Rights of the Unborn

But what about the unborn—do they have any rights under the Constitution? This is one of the most complex questions surrounding abortion. When the Supreme Court legalized abortion, it essentially ruled that the right of a woman to make private decisions about her body overruled the rights of the fetus growing inside of her, at least until the fetus was around 24–28 weeks old. At this point, the Court determined, the fetus is capable of surviving outside the mother should it be born prematurely and thus deserves more protection under the law.

But in some cases, the unborn have rights earlier than this, especially in the event of a violent crime committed against a pregnant woman. In a 2007 Texas case, for example, the state's highest criminal court ruled that the death of a fetus can be prosecuted as murder, even if the fetus is too young to survive outside the womb. The court came to this decision after it ruled that Antwonyia Smith, who shot his girlfriend while she was six weeks pregnant, could be prosecuted for a double murder. In this case, the life of the fetus was deemed as much of a loss as the life of the woman.

> **Under the U.S. Constitution, because a fetus is not yet a legal person, it cannot enjoy the same rights as the living—and thus is the property of the woman in which it resides and is subject to her decisions.**

Texas is one of 37 states that as of 2008 have laws that say that in some circumstances, the unlawful killing of an unborn child is homicide. These laws make it a separate offense to kill a fetus when a pregnant woman is injured or murdered. In 2004 President George W. Bush signed the Unborn Victims of Violence Act into law, making the federal government also capable of prosecuting someone for the murder of a fetus. Said Bush when he signed the act, "Any time an expectant mother is a victim of violence, two lives are in the balance, each deserving protection, and each deserving justice. If the crime is murder and the unborn child's life ends, justice demands a full accounting under the law."[30] Indeed, the loss of an unborn baby to violence is a crime that many people agree is worthy of harsh punishment.

However, those in the pro-choice camp worry that laws that grant a fetus such rights could eventually be used to chip away at a woman's right to access abortion. Fetal homicide laws in 24 states (and the federal government) describe a fetus as a "person." In all of these circumstances, courts specified that protecting a fetus from homicide does not conflict with the right of a woman to seek an abortion. But if a fetus can be considered a "person" with intact rights, it could one day be argued that abortion violates those rights. As Massachusetts senator John Kerry put it, "I have serious concerns about [the 2004 Unborn Victims of Violence Act] because the law cannot simultaneously provide that a fetus is a human being and protect the right of the mother to choose to terminate her pregnancy."[31] As of 2008 fetal homicide laws had not been successfully used to challenge a woman's right to access abortion, perhaps because of the understanding that a woman has a right to make decisions about her body that a third party, such as a murderer, has no right to make.

> If a fetus can be considered a 'person' with intact rights, it could one day be argued that abortion is a violation of those rights.

Does Legal Make It More Common?

After *Roe v. Wade*, it was of great concern that legalization would cause abortion to become so common that women would rely on the procedure as a gruesome form of birth control. And in fact, the U.S. abortion rate skyrocketed after 1973. According to economist Steven Levitt and writer Stephen Dubner, after *Roe v. Wade*, "conceptions rose by nearly 30 percent, but births actually *fell* by 6 percent, indicating that many women were using abortion as a method of birth control, a crude and drastic sort of insurance policy."[32] Of the high abortion rate David O'Steen, executive director of the National Right to Life Committee, says, "At one time, we were aborting one of every three pregnancies in this country. . . . If you step back and consider this, that the richest people that have ever lived on the face of this earth have somehow engaged in killing one of every three of their own offspring, you have to think something is bad."[33]

But data from around the world indicate no relationship exists between the legality and frequency of abortion. In some places where abortion is banned—like South and Central America—the illegal abortion rate is very high. On the other hand, the Netherlands, where abortion is legal, has one of the lowest abortion rates in the world. Abortion rates tend to be lower in western Europe than in eastern Europe, but abortion is legal in both places. And the United States has one of the highest abortion rates in the world. Writer Nina Kohl makes sense of the disparity in the following way: "Abortions are low in countries where women have the prevention resources [birth control] and parenting support they need to help them avoid abortions, and the abortion rate is high in countries where women don't have access to those resources."[34]

With this in mind, pro-choice advocates such as writer Kira Cochrane reject the idea that women will use abortion as a method of birth control. "Given a choice between using a condom or taking the pill and a trip to an abortion clinic, the former options obviously seem preferable."[35] A study by the Guttmacher Institute found that women who have more than one abortion are more likely to have been using either the birth control pill or an injected birth control medication when they became pregnant, which seems to refute the notion that women rely on abortion as a method of birth control. "Rather," writes women's health analyst Susan A. Cohen, "it suggests that women having abortions—especially those having more than one—are trying hard to avoid unintended pregnancy, but are having trouble doing so."[36]

Legal and Safe

Just because abortion was illegal before 1973 does not mean women did not have them. Thousands of abortions took place every year—but because there were criminal consequences, abortions were performed in a clandestine underworld that was dangerous for both patient and physician. Abortions were performed in motel rooms, basements, cars, and other environments inappropriate for surgery. Women receiving abortions in such places were prone to infection and life-threatening complications, and doctors could be arrested and stripped of their license to practice medicine if caught. Remembers one abortion rights advocate, "There were also doctors without proper training who were able to exploit women by demanding large sums of money."[37]

Because abortion doctors were hard to find and difficult to trust, many women attempted to perform abortions themselves, at great consequence to their health. Horror stories abound of women inserting objects such as hangers into their vaginal tract in an attempt to pierce the gestational sac and abort the pregnancy. The risks of such an action were infertility, infection, and death. "I once took care of a young woman who had attempted to terminate her pregnancy by injecting a solution of Lysol and bleach into her system," remembers Faye Wattleton, former president of Planned Parenthood. "She died."[38] Antiabortionists point out that the number of deaths prior to *Roe* has been greatly exaggerated by pro-choice advocates, who cite numbers as high as 5,000–10,000. In reality, only hundreds of deaths occurred per year prior to the legalization of abortion—yet for some, that is hundreds too many.

> " Data from around the world indicate no relationship exists between the legality and frequency of abortion. "

Legalizing abortion had the effect of standardizing it. Abortion doctors practice in safe, well-equipped, sterile clinics and follow a professional procedure taught in medical school. For this reason, abortion-related death rates in the United States fell after 1973, and in the twenty-first century, death and even severe complication from abortion are almost unheard of. In fact, according to the Guttmacher Institute, death during childbirth—which is also very rare in contemporary America—is 10 times more likely than death from an abortion.

The risks inherent in illegal abortion is a main reason supporters argue it must remain legal. Abortion advocates believe that women will continue to need abortions whether the procedure is legal or not, and point to statistics from countries where abortion is illegal to make their case. Indeed, according to the World Health Organization, nearly half of the world's 50 million abortions—about 19 million—are illegal, and cause the death of about 68,000 women each year. In Africa alone, an estimated 30,000 women die from botched or self-induced abortions, and hundreds of thousands are hospitalized each year. "Where abortion remains illegal and clandestine," says women's health analyst Susan A. Cohen, "women are still paying the ultimate price."[39] Therefore, those who favor the legality of abortion see it as a women's health and safety issue, in addition to a privacy one.

Whether abortion should remain legal is a question hotly debated in all corners of American society. But what should not to be forgotten is that even as a legal option, abortion is rarely a celebrated event. "Sometimes the triumphant talk of rights has overshadowed the complex responsibility women feel," said one woman who had an abortion. "Having the right doesn't make the decision any easier."[40]

Should Abortion Be Legal?

> **She doesn't want to have an abortion, but she doesn't want to have a baby. That's what I think people need to understand. You can be ambivalent about abortion and still decide to have one. And you can be ambivalent about abortion and still be pro-choice. Lots of people are.**

—Renee Chelian, quoted in Anna Quindlen, "The Clinic: A No-Spin Zone," *Newsweek*, October 16, 2006.

Chelian runs the Northland Family Planning Center, an abortion and family planning clinic in Michigan.

> **Is it really possible to 'personally oppose abortion,' support *Roe*, and still claim to be 'pro-life'? Of course not!**

—"The Case for Life and Against Pro-Abortion Disinformation," *National Right to Life News*, February 2006.

National Right to Life News is a publication of National Right to Life, an organization that opposes abortion on the grounds that it is murder.

Bracketed quotes indicate conflicting positions.

* Editor's Note: While the definition of a primary source can be narrowly or broadly defined, for the purposes of Compact Research, a primary source consists of: 1) results of original research presented by an organization or researcher; 2) eyewitness accounts of events, personal experience, or work experience; 3) first-person editorials offering pundits' opinions; 4) government officials presenting political plans and/or policies; 5) representatives of organizations presenting testimony or policy.

66 In the early 1990s, just as the first cohort of children born after *Roe v. Wade* was hitting its late teen years—the years during which young men enter their criminal prime—the rate of crime began to fall. What this cohort was missing, of course, were the children who stood the greatest chance of becoming criminals. And the crime rate continued to fall as an entire generation came of age minus the children whose mothers had not wanted to bring a child into the world. Legalized abortion led to less unwantedness; unwantedness leads to high crime; legalized abortion, therefore, led to less crime. 99

—Steven D. Levitt and Stephen J. Dubner, *Freakonomics.* New York: HarperCollins, 2005.

Levitt is a professor of economics at the University of Chicago. Dubner is a journalist whose articles have appeared in *Time* magazine and the *New Yorker*.

66 Even if abortion did lower crime by culling out 'unwanted' children, this effect would be greatly outweighed by the rise in crime associated with the greater incidence of single-parent families that also follows from abortion liberalization. In short, more abortions have brought more crime. 99

—John R. Lott, "Abortion and Crime: One Has an Effect on the Other, but It May Not Be the Effect You Think," *National Review*, August 13, 2007.

Lott is a senior research scientist at the University of Maryland and the author of the book *Freedomnomics.*

66 Isn't it strange that [a] woman could have taken the life of her unborn child and it was abortion, not murder, but if somebody else does it, that's murder? 99

—Ronald Reagan, comments during the October 27, 1984, Louisville, Kentucky, presidential election debate with Walter Mondale.

Reagan was president of the United States from 1981 to 1989.

"A pregnant woman and her fetus should never be regarded as separate, independent, and even adversarial, entities. Yet that is precisely what some antichoice organizations, legal theorists, legislators, prosecutors, doctors, and courts have attempted to do in the past decade. They have tried to build support for the notion that the fetus has legal rights independent of the woman carrying it in her womb. Although this concept is sometimes put forward in very sympathetic contexts, it is laced with risks for women's rights.**"

—"What's Wrong with Fetal Rights," American Civil Liberties Union, July 31, 1996.

The American Civil Liberties Union works to protect the civil liberties of Americans and is active on issues such as the death penalty, immigration, racism, and abortion.

"It stands to reason that a society that gives mothers the right to kill their children until birth will suffer from higher instances of child abuse.**"

—Scott Schaeffer-Duffy, "Christians Must Reject All Killing," *National Catholic Reporter*, February 23, 2007, p. 19.

Schaeffer-Duffy is a member of the Sts. Francis & Therese Catholic Worker community in Worcester, Massachusetts.

"We can acknowledge that access to abortion is a social good while acknowledging that it's a bad experience for an individual woman to have.**"

—Ann Furedi, "Some Messages Can't Be Massaged," *Conscience*, Winter 2006–2007.

Furedi is the chief executive of the British Pregnancy Advisory Service (BPAS), the United Kingdom's largest independent abortion provider.

> "We cannot forget the stories that came before, of women receiving abortions in apartments, motel rooms, in the back seats of cars. We cannot forget the quiet shame, confusion or fear that accompanied successful illegal abortions. And, we cannot close our eyes to the haunting image of a dead mother, sister, aunt, daughter, friend, or lover abandoned on a motel room floor. All of our stories are compelling reasons to keep abortion legal and safe."

—Sarah Nelson, "The Partial Birth Abortion Ban—Effects on Women's Rights, Up Close & Personal," *Women's Health Activist*, July/August 2007.

Nelson is a women's health advocate affiliated with the National Women's Health Network, a nonprofit pro-choice organization that publishes the journal *Women's Health Activist*.

> "I need to refute misconceptions, mistakes or lies that claim that since with illegal abortion (back street, coat hangers, pregnant women die in huge numbers) we have to leave the current stats of abortion as untouched. . . . The number of deaths from illegal abortion was declining markedly prior to abortion being legalized. . . . From the Atlanta-based Centers for Disease Control U.S.A.: 1940—1,682 deaths; 1950—316 deaths; 1962—205 deaths; 1970—128 deaths."

—Patrick Coffey, "Maternal Deaths from Illegal Abortion," *Catholic Insight*, January 2007.

Coffey is a physician who lives in Newcastle, Ontario.

> "Throughout history, women have had unplanned and unwanted pregnancies. And throughout history, women have found ways to terminate those pregnancies. But what has not always been guaranteed is whether they can do so legally, with the medical care necessary to protect their health."

—Elizabeth Schulte, "Is the Past a Prologue for the Roberts-Alito Court? Abortion Before *Roe*," Counterpunch.org, January 20, 2006.

Schulte is a writer for the *Socialist Worker*.

66 **Abortion is regrettable, and needs to be minimized, for the same reason that abortion is wrong and unjust: because it kills an innocent human being. That is also the reason it should be prohibited.** 99

—Ramesh Ponnuru, "Winning, and Losing, on Abortion: How Go the Wars?" *National Review*, May 8, 2006.

Ponnuru is the author of *Party of Death: The Democrats, the Media, the Courts, and the Disregard for Human Life.*

66 **Criminalization would reduce, but by no means eliminate, abortion's incidence, and that might come at a price too high for most Americans to bear.** 99

—Susan A. Cohen, "Toward Making Abortion 'Rare': The Shifting Battleground over the Means to an End," *Guttmacher Policy Review*, vol. 9, no. 1, Winter 2006.

Cohen is director of government affairs at the Guttmacher Institute, a nonprofit organization focused on sexual and reproductive health research, policy analysis, and public education.

Facts and Illustrations

Should Abortion Be Legal?

- Abortion became **legal in 1973** when the Supreme Court struck down Texas laws against abortion in the landmark case *Roe v. Wade*.

- Since *Roe v. Wade*, the U.S. Supreme Court has given more than **20 major rulings** regarding abortion.

- American women have had more than **46 million** abortions since 1973.

- In 2007, there were just under **1.3 million** abortions.

- According to the Guttmacher Institute:
  - Abortion is legal but rare in Belgium, Germany, and the Netherlands, where there are about **7, 8,** and **9 abortions per 1,000** reproductive-aged women, respectively.
  - Abortion is illegal but common in the Dominican Republic, Uganda, and Peru, where there are **47, 54,** and **56 abortions per 1,000** reproductive-aged women, respectively.

- According to the United Nations, almost **50 million** abortions occur worldwide every year. About **20 million** of these occur illegally, resulting in the deaths of about **68,000** women. Of these deaths, **30,000** (about 44 percent) take place in Africa.

Most Americans Favor Legal Abortion

The majority of Americans have supported a woman's right to access abortion services since it became legal in 1973.

Do you think abortions should be legal under any circumstances, legal only under certain circumstances, or illegal in all circumstances?

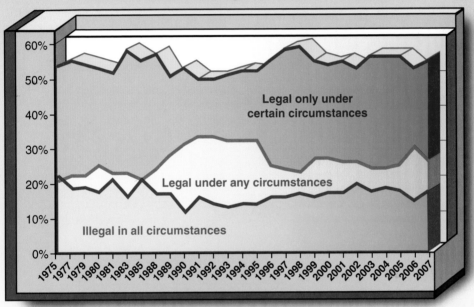

Source: Gallup poll, June 2007. www.gallup.com.

- Romania has the highest abortion rate in the world, where **75 percent** of all pregnancies end in abortion.

- In the United States, about **24 percent** of all pregnancies end in abortion.

- According to the Guttmacher Institute, **less than 0.3 percent** of abortion patients experience a complication that requires hospitalization, and a woman is **10 times** more likely to die in childbirth than to die from an abortion.

Legal vs. Illegal—Abortions Around the World

Abortion rates tend to be higher in countries where abortion is illegal than in countries where it is legal. Because illegal abortion must take place in secret, they are performed under dirty, dangerous, and unprofessional conditions and cause the death of nearly 70,000 women each year.

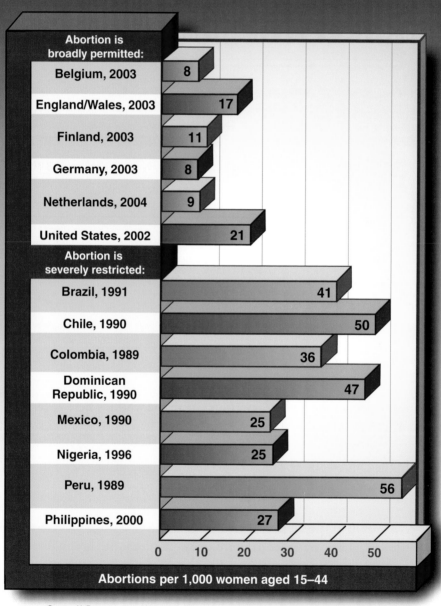

Abortion is broadly permitted:

Country	Abortions per 1,000 women aged 15–44
Belgium, 2003	8
England/Wales, 2003	17
Finland, 2003	11
Germany, 2003	8
Netherlands, 2004	9
United States, 2002	21

Abortion is severely restricted:

Country	Abortions per 1,000 women aged 15–44
Brazil, 1991	41
Chile, 1990	50
Colombia, 1989	36
Dominican Republic, 1990	47
Mexico, 1990	25
Nigeria, 1996	25
Peru, 1989	56
Philippines, 2000	27

Abortions per 1,000 women aged 15–44

Source: H. Boonstra et al., "Abortion in Women's Lives," New York: Guttmacher Institute, 2006.

Unsafe Abortion in the Developing World

According to the World Health Organization, 98 percent of all unsafe abortions take place in developing countries. The risk of dying from an unsafe abortion in a developing country is 1 in 250 procedures, while in developed countries it is 1 in 3,700 procedures. In the United States, the risk of dying is 1 in 1 million.

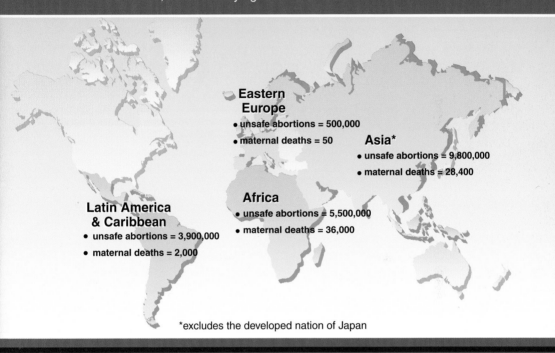

Eastern Europe
- unsafe abortions = 500,000
- maternal deaths = 50

Asia*
- unsafe abortions = 9,800,000
- maternal deaths = 28,400

Africa
- unsafe abortions = 5,500,000
- maternal deaths = 36,000

Latin America & Caribbean
- unsafe abortions = 3,900,000
- maternal deaths = 2,000

*excludes the developed nation of Japan

Source: *Global and Regional Estimates of Incidence and Mortality Due to Unsafe Abortion, 2003*. Geneva: World Health Organization, 2007.

- The risk of dying in a surgical abortion in the United States is about **1 in 1 million**.

- According to mortality reports from the Centers for Disease Control and Prevention, there have been between **4 and 12 deaths** from legal or illegal abortion every year for the past 10 years in the United States.

- The earliest baby to ever survive was delivered in 2007 in Miami, Florida. She was **21 weeks and 6 days** old (full-term pregnancies last 38–40 weeks).

Legalization Safer for Women

The number of deaths from abortion has declined dramatically since *Roe v. Wade*. Before the unprecedented legal decision of 1973, deaths from abortions were in the hundreds annually. Since the late 1970s, the number of deaths has been below 20 per year.

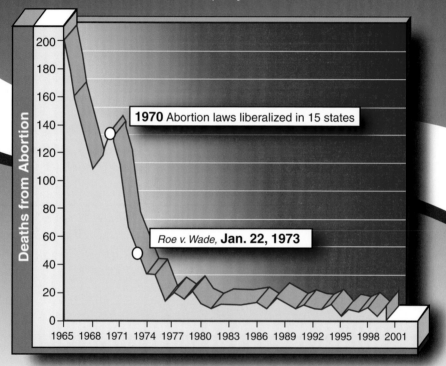

Deaths from Abortion

1970 Abortion laws liberalized in 15 states

Roe v. Wade, **Jan. 22, 1973**

Source: H. Boonstra et al., "Abortion in Women's Lives," New York: Guttmacher Institute, 2006.

- According to the Center for Reproductive Rights:
  - More than **60 percent** of the world's population lives in countries where abortion is legal.
  - More than **50 countries** allow abortion until at least the twelfth week of pregnancy.
  - Some nations, such as Britain, allow abortion through **week 24**.
  - Some nations, such as China, and some states in the United States, **have no limit**.

- A **2005 study** undertaken by the British government quantified the effects of making abortion illegal, finding that if abortion were to become outlawed in that country, it would, per year:
  - cost **750 million** pounds (about 1.5 billion U.S. dollars) in public resources;
  - cause up to **15 deaths**;
  - produce **15,000** additional teenage mothers; and
  - cause **12,000** children to be raised in neglected or abusive homes.

- The risk of death associated with abortion increases with the length of pregnancy, from 1 death for every 1 million abortions performed before the ninth week of pregnancy, to **1 per 29,000** at 16–20 weeks and **1 per 11,000** at 21 or more weeks.

- According to Gallup polls that tracked American opinions of abortion over a 30-year period:
  - **Sixty percent** of Americans consistently believe abortion should be legal in the first trimester of pregnancy.
  - **Twenty-five percent** believe abortion should be legal in the second trimester of pregnancy.
  - **Ten percent** believe abortion should be legal in the third trimester of pregnancy.

- According to the National Opinion Research Center, **80–90 percent** of Americans believe abortion should be available to a woman if she became pregnant due to rape, if her health is threatened, or if her fetus is severely deformed.

- As of 2008, **37 states** have fetal homicide laws. These are: Alabama, Alaska, Arizona, Arkansas, California, Florida, Georgia, Idaho, Illinois, Indiana, Iowa, Kansas, Kentucky, Louisiana, Maine, Maryland, Massachusetts, Michigan, Minnesota, Mississippi, Missouri, Nebraska, Nevada, North Carolina, North Dakota, Ohio, Oklahoma, Pennsylvania, Rhode Island, South Carolina, South Dakota, Tennessee, Texas, Utah, Virginia, Washington, and Wisconsin. At least **15 states** have fetal homicide laws that apply beginning at conception.

What Restrictions Should Be Placed on Abortion?

66Legislative actions such as parental notice and/or consent laws, . . . legislation seeking to make women aware of the pain unborn children may feel in an abortion, [and] laws seeking to have women considering abortion shown sonograms of their unborn child . . . serve to reduce the number of abortions and save lives.99

—Dennis Day, treasurer of the National Right to Life Committee.

66These are not decisions to be left to politicians in Washington, D.C. These are decisions that should be made by a woman, in consultation with her doctor, her family and her conscience.99

—Whitney Hoyt, political director of NARAL Pro-Choice California.

Only about a fifth of the population supports unlimited, unrestricted abortion; an even smaller group rejects abortion entirely. Instead, it is more common for Americans to support a woman's right to access abortion when it is governed by certain rules or restrictions. U.S. states gained the right to impose restrictions on abortion after the 1992 Supreme Court case *Planned Parenthood v. Casey*. From state to state, support varies for restrictions on a woman's right to access abortion, such as making her go through waiting periods, undergo mandatory counseling, receive parental notification or consent, and abide by limits that govern late-term abortion.

Mandatory Waiting Periods

One popular restriction that has been imposed on abortion services is mandatory waiting periods. As of 2008, 24 states had mandatory waiting periods that range from 1 hour (South Carolina) to 18 hours (Indiana) to 24 hours (22 other states). The purpose of imposing a waiting period is to give a pregnant woman time to mull over her decision to ensure she does not abort her pregnancy rashly or experience extreme remorse. A 2005 study by a Florida State University law professor found that mandatory waiting periods for abortion reduce female suicide rates anywhere between 10 and 30 percent. For this reason, support for mandatory waiting periods tends to be high, with around 78 percent of Americans favoring them.

But from another perspective, mandatory waiting periods can interfere with a woman's right to access abortion services. A 24-hour waiting period often requires that two trips be made to an abortion clinic—the first for an exam, the second 24 hours later for the procedure. Considering that 87 percent of the nation's population lives in counties that do not have a clinic, and 25 percent of women travel 50 miles or more to get to a clinic, 2 trips spanning 200 miles in two days can be very time-consuming and costly, especially for young and poor women. As one author put it, "Mandatory waiting periods

> **" Americans support a woman's right to access abortion when it is governed by certain rules or restrictions. "**

may require a woman to miss extra days of work because she must go to the clinic not once, but twice, to obtain an abortion. If travel is required, this can make the whole procedure unaffordable. In other words, for millions of women, youth, race, and economic circumstances together with the lack of accessible services—especially for later abortions—translate into daunting barriers, forcing some women to resort to unsafe and illegal abortions and self-abortions."[41] Those who oppose mandatory waiting periods view them as an unconstitutional obstacle to a woman's right to access abortion services.

Mandatory Counseling

Hand-in-hand with mandatory waiting periods are mandatory counseling sessions, which are required by 32 states as of 2008. States vary in what women should be counseled about, but in general all are designed to give a pregnant woman information with which she may reconsider abortion. Like mandatory waiting periods, some aspects of mandatory counseling are popular—88 percent of Americans, for example, favor laws requiring doctors to inform patients about alternatives to abortion before performing the procedure. Seventeen states require that women be given information about these alternatives, such as adoption. Twenty-one states require that women be informed that if they choose to have their child, state programs may be able to financially assist them.

> " Waiting periods give a pregnant woman time to mull over her decision to ensure she does not abort her pregnancy rashly or experience extreme remorse. "

Yet some forms of counseling are perceived as manipulative or inaccurate, and thus are frequently debated, most often in the form of initiatives on state ballots. For example, some states require that women considering abortion be shown pictures of a fetus at different stages of development. This technique is intended to underscore an idea that a pregnant woman is carrying a child that deserves to live—but this is a perspective that conflicts with other beliefs about fetal development and a woman's right to choose.

Other controversial counseling techniques include programs used in Texas, Kansas, and Minnesota, which require women to be told about a link between abortion and an increased risk of developing breast cancer. But both the American Cancer Society and the National Cancer Institute have published reports that confirm no such link. Finally, six states require that a pregnant woman be told that a fetus may be able to feel pain, which has also been hotly contested and disproved by several major studies. These discrepancies cause many to worry about the quality of information given at these mandatory counseling services—especially since many of the materials used are not produced by a state organization and could be reflecting the agenda and ideology of a private organization.

Parental Involvement Laws

Another controversial set of restriction laws are those that require that minors seeking an abortion tell or get their parents' consent. These parental notification or parental consent laws are, as of 2008, applicable in 35 states, though they vary in their requirements. Some states require teens to simply notify one or both parents; other states require teens to get written consent from one or both parents.

Parental involvement laws are popular with Americans. According to a December 2005 Gallup poll, 78 percent of Republicans, 71 percent of Independents, and 59 percent of Democrats support them, and for several reasons. Some, such as Peter Wolfgang, director of public policy at the Family Institute of Connecticut, believe that "parents have a right to know if their minor daughter is about to go through major, potentially life-altering surgery."[42] Others believe that a parent must be present to help his or her child with what could be one of the biggest decisions of the child's life. As one parent put it, "If society allows children below 18 to decide whether or not to murder their unborn babies, why should parents be responsible for them at all? Is there a bigger decision they will have to make someday?"[43]

> Those who oppose mandatory waiting periods view them as an unconstitutional obstacle to a woman's right to access abortion services.

Furthermore, there is a medical rationale for parental notification laws. As with any medical procedure, it is important to get a patient's medical history, which many teens do not know. One gynecologist supports parental involvement laws for this very reason. "I rely heavily on parents for medical history, since most girls do not know their own history," she said. "Furthermore, 95 percent of abortions are not performed by a young girl's primary care physician, but by a complete stranger who has never cared for her and will never see her again."[44] When the doctor is unfamiliar with a medical history, the patient must provide it. In addition, post-abortion care can also be aided by a parent's involvement, and is more likely to be received if a parent can take a teen to follow-up appointments and make sure she recovers well from the procedure.

Are Parental Laws Necessary?

But parental involvement laws have, in some states, been shown to have no effect on teen abortion rates and, in other states, actually threaten teens' safety. According to the Guttmacher Institute, parental involvement laws are unnecessary because 6 in 10 teenagers who have an abortion tell at least one parent anyway. A different study undertaken by the University of California, San Francisco, found that pregnant teenagers who are not forced by law to involve their parents in their decisions do so at about the same rate as teens who are required by law. About 65.3 percent of teens in Minnesota (which has a parental notification law) notified their parents, versus 62.1 percent of teens in Wisconsin (which does not). This data indicates that teens are already talking to their parents about their pregnancies without the government forcing them to.

> " Thirty-five states have parental involvement laws that require teens to simply notify one or both parents; other states require teens to get written consent from one or both parents. "

Furthermore, parental involvement laws create an obstacle for teens seeking abortion. Notifying their parents or waiting for their consent ends up delaying the procedure for many teens, which can jeopardize their health and be a more expensive procedure. Teens in Mississippi, for example, became 10–20 percent more likely to have a second-trimester abortion after that state adopted parental consent laws, according to University of California, San Francisco, researchers. In addition, the researchers found that many teens bypass parental involvement laws by going to nearby states that do not have them. Teens from Pennsylvania tend to go to New Jersey and New York to obtain abortions. Similarly, pregnant teens from Massachusetts go to neighboring Vermont, while teens in Wisconsin, Indiana, and Missouri go to nearby Illinois.

When Parental Involvement Threatens Pregnant Teens

But the biggest reason people oppose parental involvement laws is when they might put a teen at risk for hurting herself or being hurt by her family. Opponents of such laws say that forcing teens who come from abusive homes to tell their parents they are pregnant jeopardizes their safety. As Susan Nielsen, associate editor of the Portland newspaper the *Oregonian*, puts it, these teens "know darn well they can't tell their parents, perhaps because their parents are drunks or drug addicts or controlling jerks, and they've gotten beaten up or called names for much lesser offenses than an unplanned pregnancy."[45]

Furthermore, if a teen is pregnant due to rape or incest, requiring her to tell her parents could result in her own death. This happened to Spring Adams, a 13-year-old Idaho girl who became pregnant after her father raped her. When the state required her to get parental permission, her father shot and killed her, fearing she would tell someone she was pregnant with his child. All states with parental involvement laws have some form of judicial bypass, in which a teen who fears the reaction of her family can get a judge to approve an abortion without parental involvement. Yet pediatrician Richard Pan is among those skeptical of the judicial bypass option, saying, "We all know that's unrealistic. A frightened, pregnant teen is unlikely to find a courthouse and go through a legal proceeding to do this."[46]

> " Parental involvement laws have, in some states, been shown to have no effect on teen abortion rates and, in other states, threaten teens' safety. "

Even girls who come from loving homes may resort to hurting themselves out of shame of getting pregnant. They may be too embarrassed to tell their parents or fear disappointing them. Indeed, many pregnant teenagers have died after swallowing chemicals to make them abort; still others have committed suicide, indicating they would literally rather die than tell their families of their mistake. Nielsen sums up the situation in the following way: "Some of these girls merely think they can't tell their parents . . . [and are] at risk for doing something stupid. Like sneaking off to [another state like] Washington, which lacks a parental-involvement law. Or forcing a home miscarriage, using tips from the Internet. Or committing suicide to solve the problem."[47] For these reasons, the American Medical Association, the Society for Adolescent Medicine, the American Public Health Association, the American College of Obstetricians and Gynecologists, the American Academy of Pediatrics have all officially opposed parental involvement laws on the grounds that they do more harm than good to America's pregnant teens.

> " If a teen is pregnant due to rape or incest, requiring her to tell her parents could result in her own death. "

Late-Term Abortion

A final set of laws that restrict abortion are those that cover late-term abortion, or abortions that occur in the second trimester and beyond (after 12 weeks). Federally, there is no limit on when a woman can have an abortion, but just 14 states—Alaska, Hawaii, Mississippi, New Hampshire, and New Jersey, to name a few—have no laws that restrict when a woman can abort. The other 36 states have a variety of different laws on when abortion is banned (though all of them allow a late-term abortion in case the life or health of the mother is endangered by the pregnancy). Some, such as Georgia, Iowa, and Texas, prohibit abortions in the third trimester (after 24 weeks); others, such as North Carolina, prohibit after 20 weeks.

Twenty-three states restrict abortions at what is called "viability," or when a fetus is able to stay alive outside of the womb. The issue of viability can be confusing, as there is no particular week of pregnancy that all fetuses are viable. Babies born at 20 weeks usually cannot survive—some live for an hour or so before dying—but viability increases with each week thereafter. In 2007, the world record for the youngest person ever born was broken by Amillia Taylor, who was born in Miami at just 21 weeks and 6 days. Taylor has survived, though most babies her age would not. Says Dr. Phuket Tantavit, who specializes in neonatology, "Survival of babies that are less than 22 weeks of gestation is close to zero, if not zero."[48]

Certain individuals have survived long-term if born at 22 weeks, and about 33 percent of all premature babies born at 23 weeks survive. Fifty percent of all 24-week premature infants survive if they are cared for in a neonatal ICU, and viability increases through week 28, when the survival rate reaches 95 percent. Because every individual is different, no court has ruled on what week viability takes place. But states use the standard of viability to determine on a case-by-case basis whether an abortion at this late stage should be allowed or prohibited.

> **Many pregnant teenagers have died after swallowing chemicals to make them abort; still others have committed suicide, indicating they would literally rather die than tell their families of their mistake.**

Late-term abortions are controversial because the older the fetus, the closer it is to life, which makes the prospect of ending that life more upsetting to people. But despite the emotional impact they carry, late-term abortions account for the minority of all abortions—according to the Centers for Disease Control and Prevention, only 1.4 percent of abortions take place after 20 weeks.

The women who elect late-term abortions usually do so for three main reasons. They may have discovered their fetus has a life-threatening genetic deformity, such as the potential to be born without a face, limbs, or brain. Tests to discover these genetic maladies are usually not available until 14 to 18 weeks of pregnancy, making any resulting abortion occur in the late-term range. A second reason women elect to abort late-term is if their health is threatened by the pregnancy or if they develop a secondary health issue (one woman, for example, was diagnosed with cancer during her pregnancy and had to abort because the chemotherapy she needed to treat the cancer would deform the baby). Finally, poor women and young women tend to have trouble raising money and traveling to abortion clinics. These obstacles cause them to delay their abortions into the second trimester.

Partial-Birth Abortion

In April 2007, the Supreme Court, for the first time since *Roe v. Wade*, outlawed a type of late-term abortion procedure popularly known as "partial-birth abortion." In this procedure, which is medically called a "dilation and extraction," or D&X, a fetus is pulled partially out of the birth canal before being destroyed. The ban was controversial for several reasons, most of all because it was the first restriction to be upheld on abortion that does not include an exception for the health or life of the mother.

The procedure is indeed unpleasant-sounding. As one author put it, "In partial-birth abortion, a fetus is partially removed from the womb; its skull is punctured; its brains—sorry, it's 'intracranial contents'—are sucked out; and then the whole body is removed from the womb. The Constitution cannot plausibly be read to create a right to obtain this procedure."[49] On the other hand, the American College of Obstetricians and Gynecologists—which represents more than 90 percent of OB-GYNs in the United States—and other leading medical organizations, such as the American Medical Association, disagree. They opposed the ban on the ground that it is harmful to women's health and interferes with medical decision making.

> **The issue of viability can be confusing, as there is no particular week of pregnancy that all fetuses are viable.**

Despite the enormous controversy over the ruling—which enthralled antiabortionists who view the procedure as infanticide, and disappointed pro-choice advocates, who worry the ruling will be used to chip away at a woman's right to have other types of abortions—the technique in question has been used in only about

0.17 percent of American abortions, about 2,000 a year. Several other techniques can be used to perform late-term abortions, so the ban on partial-birth "saves not a single fetus from destruction, for it targets only a method of performing abortion,"[50] as Supreme Court justice Ruth Bader Ginsberg wrote in her dissent (she was opposed to the ban on the grounds that it threatened a woman's right under *Roe v. Wade*). Still, supporters of the ban, such as President George W. Bush, hailed it as "an affirmation of the progress we have made over the past six years in protecting human dignity and upholding the sanctity of life."[51]

Partial-birth abortion is just one abortion restriction that has been hotly debated in the years since *Roe v. Wade* legalized abortion. As long as abortion remains legal, Americans will no doubt continue to debate what, if any, restrictions on abortion are constitutional and appropriate.

Primary Source Quotes*

What Restrictions Should Be Placed on Abortion?

66 Once a woman has decided to end her pregnancy, a waiting period unnecessarily draws out what can already be an emotionally draining experience. 99

—Heather D. Boonstra et al., "Abortion in Women's Lives," Guttmacher Institute, 2006.

The authors are research analysts for the Guttmacher Institute, a nonprofit organization focused on sexual and reproductive health research, policy analysis, and public education.

66 Waiting periods induce added reflection on the part of a woman seeking an abortion. This added reflection presumably causes a woman to have less regret after having an abortion, decreasing the incidence of depression and ultimately of suicide. 99

—Jonathan Klick, "Mandatory Waiting Periods for Abortions and Female Mental Health," FSU College of Law, Law and Economics Paper no. 05-27, September 17, 2005.

Klick is a law professor at Florida State University. His empirical study of waiting periods concluded that the adoption of mandatory waiting periods for abortion reduces female suicide rates anywhere from 10 to 30 percent.

Bracketed quotes indicate conflicting positions.

* Editor's Note: While the definition of a primary source can be narrowly or broadly defined, for the purposes of Compact Research, a primary source consists of: 1) results of original research presented by an organization or researcher; 2) eyewitness accounts of events, personal experience, or work experience; 3) first-person editorials offering pundits' opinions; 4) government officials presenting political plans and/or policies; 5) representatives of organizations presenting testimony or policy.

❝Many people are affected when a teenager has an abortion without informing anyone. The father, the paternal grandparents and the maternal grandparents have a right to know the baby exists. As a parent, I have a right to know what my daughter is going through physically and emotionally.❞

—Patricia Headley, "Parental Notification Is Just Common Sense," *Champaign (IL) News Gazette*, October 4, 2006.

Headley is a parent in Ludlow, Illinois.

❝It is not unreasonable for parents to want to know what's going on with their kids. I would just suggest that parental rights have limits. Children—including teenagers—have a fundamental right to love and decent caretaking. That right sometimes conflicts with and outweighs their parents' rights to control them.❞

—Judith Warner, "When the Parents Can't Know," *New York Times*, July 29, 2006.

Warner is the author of *Perfect Madness: Motherhood in the Age of Anxiety* and a contributing columnist to the *New York Times*.

❝Girls need regular medical follow-up after an abortion to detect future complications. It is highly unlikely that a teenage girl will seek appropriate treatment for complications arising from a secret abortion, thus endangering her health. I cannot go home with the young girl, therefore the care that I can provide is limited to my office—only parents can provide care beyond that.❞

—Drea Olmstead, "Secrecy Not the Answer in Abortion Decision," *Eugene (OR) Register-Guard*, November 3, 2006.

Olmstead is a an obstetrician-gynecologist who practices in Oregon, where in 2006 voters turned down a ballot measure that would have made it mandatory for a teen to acquire parental consent for an abortion.

❝What is the intended impact of mandated parental involvement laws? If the goal was better parent-child communication, you'd expect pediatricians, child development experts, social workers, and educators to be behind them. Instead, most of the support for these laws comes from the usual suspects opposed to contraception and abortion. Good parent-child communication is a worthy goal, but putting hurdles in the way of responsible minors seeking health care is not the means of reaching it.**❞**

—Susan Lloyd Yolen, remarks at the Select Committee on Children forum, April 27, 2007.

Yolen is the vice president of public affairs and communication of Planned Parenthood of Connecticut.

❝How many of these children might have received better counseling and care under a parental notification law? How many of them were victims of statutory rape—something that would be easier to track under a parental notification law? Current law does not even require abortion providers to provide post-abortion support or care. Without a parental notification law, the minor child who goes through this life-altering procedure is left on her own.**❞**

—Peter Wolfgang, quoted in Daniela Altimari, "Should Parents Be Notified?" *Hartford (CT) Courant*, March 16, 2007.

Wolfgang is the director of public policy for the Family Institute of Connecticut.

❝As the mom of a soon-to-be teenage daughter, I want to know if my daughter is in trouble—any kind of trouble—so I can be there to help her through. But I don't believe a law forcing her to tell me is the answer.**❞**

—Cindy Richards, "Notification: It's Time to Use Good Sense," *Chicago Sun-Times*, January 24, 2007.

Richards is a mother whose columns have appeared in the *Sun-Times*.

66 Do you believe for one second that Thomas Jefferson, James Madison, and Benjamin Franklin would support a legal system that allows children alone to make decisions about elective surgery—surgery that terminates a potential human being? No rational person could believe the Founding Fathers would violate the doctrine of parental responsibility in that way. 99

—Bill O'Reilly, "Secular Progressives Keep Parents in the Dark," *Columbia (MO) Daily Tribune*, October 28, 2006.

O'Reilly is a conservative news anchor who hosts the show "The O'Reilly Factor" for Fox News.

66 [A parental notification] law would hurt not only the girls with unsupportive or abusive parents, but also the 'good girls' in the middle: They're among the teenagers who might jeopardize their health to avoid telling Mom or Dad. 99

—Susan Nielsen, "Abortion Law Hits Home for Happy Families, Too," *Portland Oregonian*, October 29, 2006.

Nielsen is the associate editor of the *Oregonian*, a newspaper based in Portland, Oregon.

66 The child is mostly delivered before the abortionist punctures the base of her skull with sharp instruments. The kids are alive when the abortionist begins the soul-chilling 'procedure' and up until the moment when the scissors or hollow metal rod is thrust deeply into the skull. If there is any small chance that a baby is still alive after that trauma, she won't be after her brains are vacuumed out. Mark this down: a premature human is deliberately pulled to within just a few inches of being a live-born person, medically and legally, even under the law of *Roe v. Wade*. That's the gruesome reality. 99

—*National Right to Life News*, "Fourteen Years of Devotion and Dedication," May 2007.

National Right to Life News is a publication of National Right to Life, an organization that opposes abortion on the grounds that it is murder.

> ❝It was reasonable for Congress to think that partial-birth abortion, more than standard D&E [dilation and extraction] 'undermines the public's perception of the appropriate role of a physician during the delivery process and perverts a process during which life is brought into the world.'❞

—Anthony Kennedy, Supreme Court majority opinion, 2007.

Kennedy has been a Supreme Court justice since 1988.

> ❝Anti-abortion groups renamed it 'partial-birth abortion,' a term that was not scientific, accurate or even coherent. They sought to blur the distinction between abortion and infanticide by making the procedure sound like an interrupted birth when, in fact, it was a second-trimester abortion. In short, the ban was conceived as a public relations tool. Even some right-to-lifers complain that it's just for show. In Congress and on television, this blurring strategy is effective. But, in courtrooms, it's disastrous.❞

—William Saletan, "Abortion Foes Let Their Zeal Trump Strategy," *Los Angeles Times*, June 4, 2004.

Saletan, chief political correspondent for the political online newsmagazine *Slate.com*, is the author of *Bearing Right: How Conservatives Won the Abortion War*.

> ❝This ban has no health exception—even if a doctor determines that a banned procedure is the safest option. Under this law, doctors could receive up to two years in prison for acting in what they believe is the best interest of their patient.❞

—Whitney Hoyt, "Abortion Ruling Trumps State Law," *Marin (CA) Independent Journal*, May 22, 2007.

Hoyt is the political director of NARAL Pro-Choice California, the political leader of the pro-choice movement.

Facts and Illustrations

What Restrictions Should Be Placed on Abortion?

- According to a May 2007 Gallup poll:

    - **Fifty-five percent** of Americans believe abortion should be legal but with restrictions and rules.

    - **Twenty-six percent** believe it should be legal under all circumstances.

    - **Eighteen percent** believe it should be illegal under all circumstances.

- In the 1970s, the majority of 28-week-old premature babies died. Technological advances have improved a 28-week-old baby's chance of surviving to **95 percent**.

- **Thirty-two states** require that women considering abortions receive counseling before the procedure.

- **Twenty-four states** require that women considering abortions wait a certain amount of time before the procedure. South Carolina has the shortest waiting period, at 1 hour. Tennessee has a 48-hour mandatory waiting period that is currently on hold pending litigation.

- **Thirty-six states** prohibit abortions after a certain point in time, except for when necessary to protect the mother's health or life. **Twenty-three states** prohibit abortions at "fetal viability." **Five states** prohibit abortions in the third trimester.

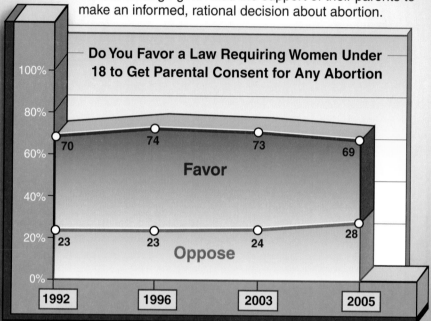

Americans Want Parental Consent for Teen Abortions

According to a Gallup poll, since 1992 support for parental consent laws has averaged around 70 percent, clearly indicating that a majority of Americans feel that teenage girls need the support of their parents to make an informed, rational decision about abortion.

Do You Favor a Law Requiring Women Under 18 to Get Parental Consent for Any Abortion

Favor

	1992	1996	2003	2005
Favor	70	74	73	69
Oppose	23	23	24	28

Source: Gallup poll, 2006. www.gallup.com.

- Teenagers account for about **19 percent** of all abortions in the United States.

- **Thirty-five states** require some level of parental involvement in a minor's decision to have an abortion. Twenty-two states require parental consent only; 11 states require parental notification only.

- All 35 states that require some level of parental involvement have a judicial bypass option, which allows a minor to obtain permission for an abortion from a court if it is determined that telling her family would endanger her health or safety. **Six states** allow a minor to receive permission from a grandparent or other relative.

- **Twenty-nine states** do not require parental permission in the event of a medical emergency. **Fourteen states** do not require parental permission when a minor has become pregnant due to rape, and/or incest.

Parental Consent Laws by State

Laws that require a teen to involve her parents in her decision to have an abortion vary from state to state. Twenty-two states require a teen to notify her parents and get their permission before she is allowed to have an abortion.

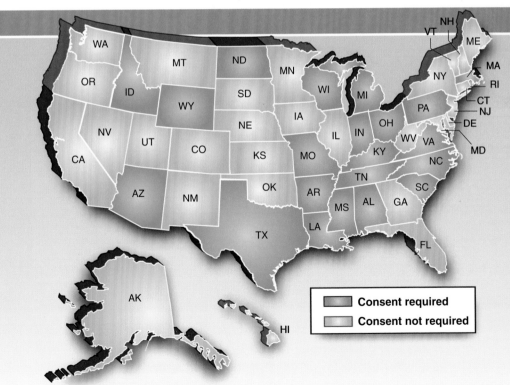

Consent required
Consent not required

Source: "State Policies in Brief: Mandatory Counseling and Waiting Periods for Abortion," Guttmacher Institute, December 1, 2007.

Americans Oppose Partial-Birth Abortion

The majority of Americans approved of the Supreme Court's 2007 decision to uphold a ban on a controversial, late-term abortion technique known as partial-birth abortion. During a partial-birth abortion the fetus is partially removed from the womb. Then a sharp object is used to pierce the skull, and a vacuum is inserted to extract the brain. The soft skull contracts and the dead fetus is easily removed from the womb.

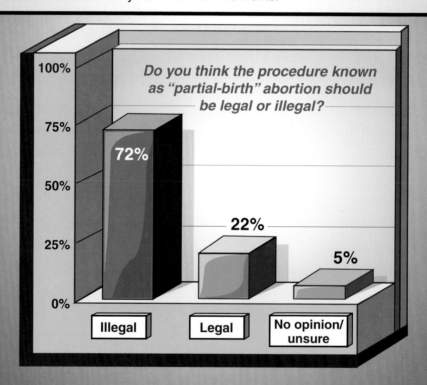

Do you think the procedure known as "partial-birth" abortion should be legal or illegal?

Illegal	72%
Legal	22%
No opinion/unsure	5%

Source: Gallup poll, May 10–13, 2007.

- A *New York Times* study that analyzed states that enacted parental involvement laws from 1995 to 2004 found **no evidence** that the laws had any **significant impact** on the number of minors who got pregnant or had abortions.

State Laws on Mandatory Counseling

Laws that require a woman to undergo counseling exist in 32 states but vary. Some states require a woman be told about alternatives to abortion; other states require a woman be informed she can receive financial help to pay for prenatal care. Laws that require women be told there is a link between breast cancer and abortion and that fetuses can feel pain are hotly contested because there is a lack of evidence supporting both claims.

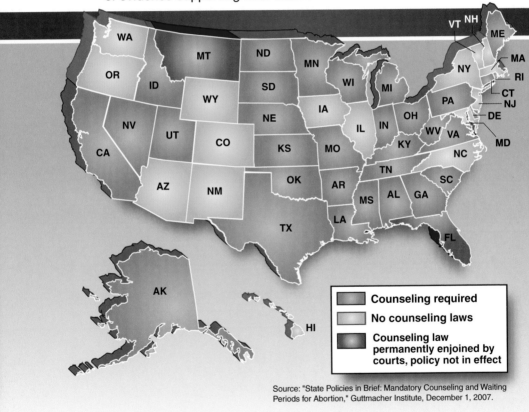

Counseling required
No counseling laws
Counseling law permanently enjoined by courts, policy not in effect

Source: "State Policies in Brief: Mandatory Counseling and Waiting Periods for Abortion," Guttmacher Institute, December 1, 2007.

- **Thirty-nine states** require an abortion to be performed by a licensed physician. **Nineteen states** require an abortion to be performed in a hospital if it is late-term. **Eighteen states** require that two physicians be involved in late-term abortions.

- According to the Guttmacher Institute, **87 percent** of the U.S. population lives in counties that do not have a clinic, and about 25 percent of women who live in these counties travel 50 miles or more to get to a clinic.

- Since *Roe v. Wade* legalized abortion in 1973, the U.S. Supreme Court has given more than **20 major rulings** modifying, informing, restricting, or regulating a woman's right to abortion.

- Women prefer to have abortions as soon as possible for emotional, financial, and health reasons. According to the Guttmacher Institute:
  - **Thirty-four percent** of women who abort at or before 6 weeks gestation would have preferred an earlier procedure.
  - **Seventy-two percent** of women who abort during 9–12 weeks would have preferred an earlier procedure.
  - **Ninety-two percent** of women who abort after 13 weeks would have preferred an earlier procedure.

What Measures Might Reduce the Need for Abortion?

❝Women don't want to need abortions.❞

—Frances Kissling, president of Catholics for a Free Choice.

❝I have never met anyone who is pro-abortion.❞

—New York senator Hillary Rodham Clinton.

Regardless whether they think abortion should be legal or not, both pro-life and pro-choice people agree that in a perfect world, no woman would need to have one. Indeed, former president Bill Clinton summed up the majority of the country's view on abortion when he famously described abortion as ideally being "safe, legal, and rare." And although the United States has one of the highest abortion rates in the developed world, abortion in America is, in general, on the decline. After becoming legal in 1973, the abortion rate peaked in 1980, when 29.3 abortions were performed per 1,000 live births. By 2003, that number had dropped to about 20.8 abortions per every 1,000 live births. Further reducing the number of abortions is a goal of both pro-choice and pro-life Americans. Several options exist as alternatives to surgical abortion that could help reduce society's need to access abortion.

The most controversial and recent alternative to surgical abortion is the so-called abortion pill, approved for use in the United States by the

Food and Drug Administration (FDA) in 2000. Once called RU-486, the abortion pill's chemical name is mifepristone, and is sold under the brand name Mifeprex. It is more commonly referred to as medical or nonsurgical abortion, or simply as the abortion pill.

The abortion pill is a steroid developed from hormones and is similar to a chemical found in birth control pills. It works by interrupting the chemical process of a pregnancy over several steps. The first step involves blocking the hormones required to develop a fetus. In the first seven weeks of pregnancy, the body produces high levels of the hormone progesterone. The abortion pill binds to progesterone receptors and blocks their uptake of the hormone. This prevents the pregnancy from progressing. Then, a second medication is given that causes the uterus to have contractions and thus forces a miscarriage.

> " **Reducing the number of abortions is a goal of both pro-choice and pro-life Americans.** "

About 90 percent of women who take this medicinal combination miscarry within 6 hours. A minority of women miscarry within the week, and a small number of women (about 0.3–0.4 percent) require a follow-up surgery in the event they do not miscarry. The earlier the pill is taken, the more effective it is. It is 99 percent effective at 7 weeks; the efficacy rate drops to 77–91 percent when taken at nine weeks, the latest point at which it can be used.

A Popular Option

Nonsurgical abortion is gaining popularity in places such as Europe, where it has been available for 2 decades. In France, more than 40 percent of all abortions are nonsurgical; women in nations such as the United Kingdom, Sweden, and Norway opt for medical abortion between 10 and 50 percent of the time. In the United States, about 9 percent of all abortions are medical.

Medical abortion is becoming favored for several reasons. First, it has a higher success rate than surgical abortion in very early pregnancies. When a woman is just a few weeks pregnant, the gestational sac (which contains the fetus) is very small, and can be difficult to find in a surgical abortion. For this reason, women usually must wait until they are more than 7 weeks pregnant to have a surgical abortion. In fact, surgical abortions performed at less than 7 weeks are 3 times more likely to fail than those performed between 7 and 12 weeks. But if a woman knows when she is 4 weeks pregnant that she wants to abort, waiting longer can be emotionally stressful. Aborting earlier in the pregnancy is generally healthier, less expensive, and medically, emotionally, and ethically less controversial than later-term abortions. The option of aborting via pill at an early stage of pregnancy is thus appealing to women looking to finalize their decision as soon as possible.

Medical abortion is also favored because it is less invasive than surgical abortion. Women who opt for the abortion pill do not have to visit an abortion clinic or cross picket lines of angry, hostile protestors to end a pregnancy. They do not have to be anesthetized, wear a hospital gown, or experience the discomfort of a clinic setting. With the abortion pill, a woman must visit her doctor or clinic to receive the medication, but then takes the medication and experiences the aftermath in the privacy and comfort of her home. For this reason, many look to the abortion pill to

> " Nonsurgical abortion is gaining popularity in places such as Europe, where it has been available for two decades. "

fulfill what one woman describes as what abortion "always should have been: a private medical matter between a woman and her doctor."[52]

Finally, nonmedical abortion could make the service more accessible to women who live in rural areas away from clinics. In the United States, just 13 percent of the nation lives in a county with an abortion clinic. The availability of a pill that can be prescribed to anyone, anywhere, however, could make abortions easier for nonurban women to obtain.

More Common or More Rare?

Yet increased availability of the abortion pill is one reason why people oppose it. Those generally against abortion worry that a pill that makes abortion more convenient will encourage women who may be deterred by the involvedness of surgical abortion to abort. Often described as "do-it-yourself" abortion, it is a concern that an abortion method that makes the procedure easier and more convenient will make fewer women think twice about having one. As George W. Bush worried when the abortion pill first became legal in the United States, "I fear that making this abortion pill widespread will make abortions more and more common, rather than more and more rare."[53]

>
> **Aborting earlier in the pregnancy is generally healthier, less expensive, and medically, emotionally, and ethically less controversial than later-term abortions.**

Yet interestingly, research shows that the convenience of the abortion pill has not led to an increased abortion rate, and in some places, it has decreased it. In Europe, the abortion rate of nations that have allowed the abortion pill for 10, 15, and even 20 years has remained stable. Some nations, such as Sweden, where more than 50 percent of all abortions are nonsurgical, have seen a reduction in the abortion rate since adding the nonsurgical option. "There is no evidence that making medical abortion available increases the overall number of abortions performed,"[54] says Dr. Terri Foran, who has studied the issues surrounding the abortion pill for Australia, a nation that has legalized the drug but has not yet developed or distributed it due to controversy.

Finally, some women attracted to the nonsurgical abortion option expect it might hurt less than surgical abortion. Yet quite the opposite is true: the cramps, pain, and bleeding that result from nonsurgical abortion tend to be more prolonged and intense than from a surgical abortion. Other side effects of the pill include headache, nausea, hemorrhaging, and in rare instances, death. A Planned Parenthood study that analyzed nonsurgical abortions between 2001 and 2004 found that 2.2 women out of every 1,000 experienced extreme bleeding, and 0.5 percent of them lost so much blood that they needed to have a blood transfusion. One American woman died from heavy bleeding—her pregnancy was ectopic, meaning the fetus was developing in the fallopian tube instead of the womb. This caused complications to arise when the abortion pill was taken and led to her death.

At least five other women have died from a bacterial infection after taking the abortion pill. The FDA and other organizations have, as of 2008, not established a causal link between the deaths and the pills, but the matter is yet to be fully investigated. Interestingly, nations in which the drug has been legal for years longer than in the United States have not experienced any deaths, leading some researchers to believe that higher American rates of pelvic inflammatory disease are responsible for the complications. Although the death rate from the abortion pill is much less than from other popular medications, such as the male potency pill Viagra, the risk has caused some to question whether it is in fact a safe and realistic alternative to surgical abortion. As one woman who experienced a severe reaction to the abortion pill said, "It's not the panacea millions of women like me thought it would be."[55]

Increasing Contraception Use

According to national statistics, about half of all American pregnancies are unintended, and about 40 percent of those end in abortion. Therefore, a sure-fire way to reduce abortion is to prevent unwanted pregnancies in the first place. In most cases, this means increasing successful birth control, or contraception, use.

Making contraception more prevalent and affordable is one way to increase its use and reduce the number of unwanted pregnancies. Indeed, poor women are less likely than wealthy women to be educated about multiple forms of birth control and able to purchase them. According to a study undertaken by the Guttmacher Institute, poor women are 4 times more likely to have an unplanned pregnancy, 3 times more likely to have an abortion, and 5 times more likely to have an unplanned birth than higher-income women. "Much in American society is not currently structured to facilitate effective contraceptive use," says woman's health advocate Cynthia Dailard. "The high cost of health care, including contraceptive supplies and services, is a major issue for many."[56] Increasing women's

> **The convenience of the abortion pill has not led to an increased abortion rate.**

access to low-cost birth control and making its use less taboo are 2 ways to facilitate that change.

However, not all unwanted pregnancies occur because a couple failed to use contraception. More often, an unwanted pregnancy that ends in abortion is the result of contraception that failed—a condom that broke or a birth control pill that was ineffective or taken improperly. Indeed, no birth control method can fully protect against pregnancy. The birth control pill has a 99 percent efficacy rate when used correctly; condoms prevent pregnancy 98 percent of the time when used correctly. As proof of how unreliable contraception can be, about 9 out of 10 women who become unexpectedly pregnant said they were using contraception at the time. In fact, just 11 percent of all sexually active women who become pregnant because they did not use birth control account for 46 percent of all abortions, according to the Guttmacher Institute.

> A sure-fire way to reduce abortion is to prevent unwanted pregnancies in the first place.

It is important that women who were unable to prevent an unwanted pregnancy with contraception be better prepared in the future. For this reason, contraception counseling is usually a part of postabortion care procedures. Following abortions that take place at Planned Parenthood and other clinics, women are educated on how to properly use contraceptives and are supplied with at least one form of birth control, such as the pill or condoms, to begin using as soon as they are healed from their procedure. This education is usually short-lived, however, as most women do not use such clinics for ongoing family planning care. Increasing the availability of this and other family planning services can limit the number of unwanted pregnancies, and thus reduce the number of abortions.

Reducing the Need for Abortion Through Sex Education

Can providing America's youth with sex education and birth control reduce its rate of unwanted pregnancy, or make sex so casual and acceptable that more unwanted pregnancies will occur? This is the question debated by American teachers, parents, politicians, and policy makers as they consider whether the need for abortion can be reduced through sex education programs in schools.

What kind of sex education should be taught, and what effect it can have on teen pregnancy, is a very controversial matter. To some, educating teens on how to use contraceptives is a way to arm them against not only unplanned pregnancies but also other dangers of unprotected sex, such as sexually transmitted disease and emotional hardship. Says publisher Kathy Clay-Little, "At its worst, the consequence of ignorance about sex can be a death sentence. At less than its worst—there is no best—its costs to society is akin to bankruptcy: children born to premature parents, the poverty that it perpetuates and the high medical and social costs."[57]

Yet others believe there is no better way to prevent teen pregnancy than by encouraging kids not to have sex in the first place—and this means teaching them to abstain from sex. Indeed, abstinence education is a popular, yet controversial, sex education message. According to a 2003 survey by National Public Radio, the Kaiser Family Foundation and Harvard University's John F. Kennedy School of Government, 30 percent of schools teaching sex education focus on abstinence only. But while it is true that abstaining from sex is the only 100 percent way to avoid becoming pregnant, it is not clear that teens who pledge to abstain from sex will follow through on that promise. A 2005 study by Yale and Columbia universities, for example, found that kids who pledge abstinence are more likely to have unsafe sex than kids who are taught to use contraception.

> " Increasing women's access to low-cost birth control and making its use less taboo are two ways to reduce the need for abortion. "

Ultimately, however, whether sex education and abstinence programs can reduce the abortion rate is somewhat moot, because a minority of abortions occur among teenagers. Indeed, only about one fifth (19 percent) of all abortions are had by pregnant teens; the vast majority are had by adult women. As analyst Susan A. Cohen says, "for most people over the course of most of their lives, it is contraceptive use that is likely to have the greatest impact"[58] on reducing abortions, rather than abstaining from sex. But teaching sex education and even abstinence at the school level can inform a young person's sexual habits once they reach adulthood, and for this reason sex education programs are typically included in legislation that seeks to reduce the number of abortions.

The Adoption Option

Finally, adoption remains an infrequently used yet viable alternative to abortion. In the early 1970s, when abortion became legal, only about 9 percent of all babies were put up for adoption. The rate fell to less than 1 percent by 1995, and has remained low. In the twenty-first century, very few babies are put up for adoption; in 2003, about 14,000 American babies were.

But antiabortion policy makers are attempting to persuade more women to place their babies for adoption rather than aborting them. This is the hope behind one piece of legislation introduced in 2006 that aims to reduce the abortion rate by 95 percent in 10 years. Called the Pregnant Women Support Act, its plan is to make it financially easier for pregnant women considering abortion to bring their babies to term. The act would provide prenatal financial and medical support for pregnant women and increase the tax credit offered to people who adopt. Some view the legislation and proadoption campaigns like it as a sensible alternative to abortion. Says one woman who put her child up for adoption, "Today I am so grateful that I was given the strength to follow through on my adoption plan, as I have witnessed how my decision has truly been best for [her birth child] Ryan and given him all I hoped for and more."[59] Yet it typically is not financially, emotionally, or professionally realistic for the majority of women who find themselves unexpectedly pregnant to carry an unwanted child to term, and thus adoption remains an underutilized alternative to abortion.

What Measures Might Reduce the Need for Abortion?

66 **Abortion is undeniably the taking of potential life. It is not pretty. It is not easy. And in a perfect world, it would not be necessary.** 99

—Bart Slepian, quoted in Amanda Robb, "Last Clinic Standing," *Marie Claire*, October 2006.

Slepian was an abortion doctor who practiced in Buffalo, New York. He was killed in 1998 by antiabortion extremists.

66 **Let us unite around a common goal of reducing the amount of abortions, not by making them illegal as many are attempting to do or overturning *Roe v. Wade* and undermining the constitutional protections that decision provided, but by preventing unintended pregnancies in the first place through education, contraception, accessible health care and services, empowering women to make decisions.** 99

—Hilary Rodham Clinton, speech at the National Family Planning and Reproductive Health Association luncheon, June 13, 2006.

Clinton is a New York senator and the former First Lady.

Bracketed quotes indicate conflicting positions.

* Editor's Note: While the definition of a primary source can be narrowly or broadly defined, for the purposes of Compact Research, a primary source consists of: 1) results of original research presented by an organization or researcher; 2) eyewitness accounts of events, personal experience, or work experience; 3) first-person editorials offering pundits' opinions; 4) government officials presenting political plans and/or policies; 5) representatives of organizations presenting testimony or policy.

❝It is time the [Australian] Government . . . gave Australian women access to a drug that 2 million users have shown to be safe and effective. RU-486 has the potential to change the world of abortion. It can be used much earlier than surgical abortion; can be dispensed by a GP [general practitioner] in the privacy of a surgery; and can give rural women, far from clinics, more equitable access to terminations.❞

—Adele Horin, "The Abortion Pill Is About Women, Not Politics," *Sydney Morning Herald*, November 12, 2005.

Horin is a reporter for the *Sydney Morning Herald* in Australia, where the abortion pill is technically legal but not yet available due to controversy.

❝Do-it-yourself abortion has no place in a civilized society.❞

—J.C. Watts Jr., quoted in "Capital Briefs," *Human Events*, October 6, 2000.

Watts is a Republican congressman from Oklahoma and chairman of the House Republican Conference.

❝We're willing to offer $200, $300, $400 on the spot, no strings attached [to help a woman considering abortion for financial reasons]. No life should end because of money.❞

—Pat Foley, quoted in Nancy Gibbs, "One Woman at a Time," *Time*, February 26, 2007.

Foley runs the Wakota Life Care Center in St. Paul, Minnesota. The center supplies pregnant women considering abortion for financial reasons with money, food, and other supplies.

❝If ethicists are serious about reducing abortions, . . . this will not be done by coercing women to bear children they feel they cannot raise but by helping women as much as possible not to become involuntarily pregnant.❞

—Rosemary Radford Ruether, "'Consistent Life Ethic' is Inconsistent," *National Catholic Reporter*, November 17, 2006.

Ruether is a professor of feminist theology at the Graduate Theological Union in Berkeley, California.

66 Most women struggle with their decision to end a pregnancy. The availability of the abortion pill does not make their *decision* easier. It may, however, make the process easier. And why should that be wrong? 99

—Ann Furedi, "What's Wrong with 'Do-It-Yourself' Abortions?" Pro-ChoiceForum.org, June 5, 2006.

Furedi is the chief executive of the British Pregnancy Advisory Service (BPAS), the United Kingdom's largest independent abortion provider.

66 You know what else would help [keep women safe regarding the abortion pill]? If doctors and clinic staff dispelled the misconception many women have that the 'early option' is an easy option. 99

—Norine Dworkin-McDaniel, "Betrayed by a Pill," *Marie Claire*, July 2007.

Dworkin-McDaniel is a pro-choice writer who experienced a severe reaction to the abortion pill.

66 Making abortion rare will require a new ethic of both individual, personal responsibility, and collective, public responsibility. It will mean improving a woman's access to the two things that can help her avoid an abortion: prevention resources and parenting support. 99

—Nina Kohl, "Making Abortion Rare," *Tikkun*, March/April 2007.

Kohl is a Milwaukee-based writer and communications consultant.

66 While it is theoretically possible that increased social supports for pregnant women and even more 'adoption-positive' problem-pregnancy counseling could have some impact, neither can hope to approach the real reductions in the abortion rate that could be achieved by preventing unintended pregnancy in the first place. 99

—Susan A. Cohen, "Toward Making Abortion 'Rare': The Shifting Battleground over the Means to an End," *Guttmacher Policy Review*, vol. 9, no. 1, Winter 2006.

Cohen is director of government affairs at the Guttmacher Institute, a nonprofit organization focused on sexual and reproductive health research, policy analysis, and public education.

66 The latest research shows that sex-education programs that promote 'safe sex' have no effect on reducing teenage sexual activity. 'Abstinence only' programs however, have cut sexual activity by over 50% in places depending on the program. . . . Safe sex is a myth. . . . Safe-sex campaigns give an appearance of moral respectability but avoid real moral accountability. 99

—Johannes L. Jacobse, "Teen Sex Is Killing Our Kids," The Crossroads Initiative, December 2007.

Jacobse is a Greek Orthodox priest and editor of the Orthodoxy Today Web site.

66 The cult of virginity that is created and perpetuated by abstinence-only education actually increases unsafe sex. A five year study of 12,000 adolescents aged 12 to 18 found that sex without protection is a third more likely among young people who signed virginity-until-marriage pledges. . . . 'It's difficult to simultaneously prepare for sex and say you're not going to have sex.' 99

—LeeChe Leong, "Virulent Virginity; 'Abstinence-Only' Sex Ed Programs Are Putting Youth at Risk," *Colorlines*, vol. 7, no. 4, January 31, 2005.

Leong is a contributor to *ColorLines*, a national, multiracial magazine devoted to the complex issues affecting communities of color.

66 For many, many years, I thought that the worst thing I'd ever done was to place my children for adoption. I thought I couldn't care for them and that was best at the time; but even so, I always thought of this as my greatest failure. After I became 100% pro-life, I realized that placing a child for adoption could be an act of great courage. 99

—Norma McCorvey, quoted in "Interview: *Canticle* talks with Miss Norma McCorvey," *Canticle*, no. 8, Winter 2000.

McCorvey was "Jane Roe" of the *Roe v. Wade* court case that legalized abortion.

Facts and Illustrations

What Measures Might Reduce the Need for Abortion?

- The **abortion pill**, or RU486, was first registered in France in 1988. Since then it has been used by between **2.5 and 5 million** women worldwide.

- As of 2008, the **abortion pill was legal** in Albania, Armenia, Australia, Austria, Azerbaijan, Belarus, Belgium, China, Cuba, Denmark, Estonia, France, Finland, Georgia, Germany, Greece, Hungary, India, Israel, Latvia, Luxembourg, Moldova, Montenegro, the Netherlands, New Zealand, Norway, Russia, Serbia, Spain, South Africa, Sweden, Switzerland, Taiwan, Tunisia, Ukraine, the United Kingdom, the United States, Uzbekistan, and Vietnam. It is also under consideration in Italy and, though legal, is awaiting distribution in Hungary and Australia.

- In 2005 the FDA rejected a request from pharmaceutical companies to make the abortion pill available over-the-counter, so it remains available in the United States by prescription only.

- Since 2000, about **650,000** American women have taken the abortion pill. Eight women in the United States, 2 women in the United Kingdom, one woman in Sweden, and one woman in Canada have died following its use.

- At least **five American women** have died from a bacterial infection that officials have not conclusively linked to the abortion pill.

- A 2007 study published in the *New England Journal of Medicine* found that abortion pills **do not reduce** a woman's chance of having a baby in the future.

- About **9 percent** of all abortions in the United States are nonsurgical, or via the abortion pill.

- About **40 percent** of all abortions in France are nonsurgical; **50 percent** in Sweden; **30 percent** in the United Kingdom.

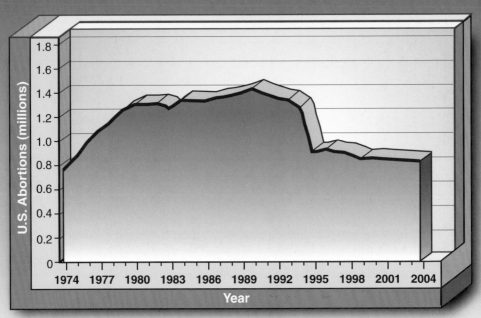

Abortion Since *Roe v. Wade*

Abortions increased sharply through the 1970s after *Roe v. Wade* legalized abortion in 1973. They peaked in the late 1980s at around 1.4 million per year. Since then abortions have declined, and in 2004 the CDC reported 830,577 legal abortions.

Source: "Abortions Surveillance–United States, 2004," *Morbidity and Mortality Weekly Report,* Centers for Disease Control and Prevention, November 23, 2007, vol. 56, no. SS-9. ww.cdc.gov.

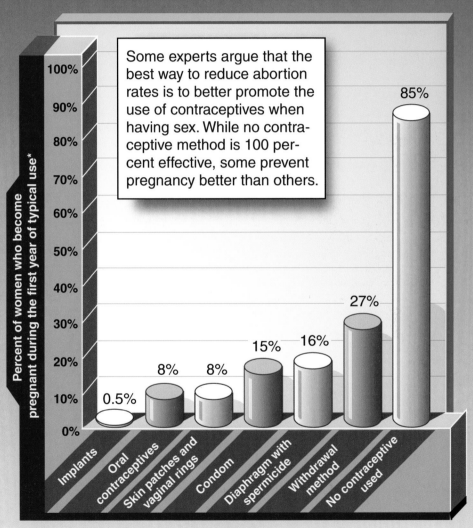

Effectiveness of Various Contraceptive Methods

Some experts argue that the best way to reduce abortion rates is to better promote the use of contraceptives when having sex. While no contraceptive method is 100 percent effective, some prevent pregnancy better than others.

Percent of women who become pregnant during the first year of typical use*

85%

27%

16%

15%

8%

8%

0.5%

Implants

Oral contraceptives

Skin patches and vaginal rings

Condom

Diaphragm with spermicide

Withdrawal method

No contraceptive used

*Typical use refers to imperfect use, such as forgetting to take a birth control pill, etc.

Source: www.merck.com.

Legalization Combined with Widely Available Contraception May Be Best for Reducing Abortion Rates

In a worldwide study conducted by the World Health Organization, the lowest abortion rates were found in western Europe where abortion is legal and contraception methods are used widely. However, in Uganda, where abortion is illegal and abstinence is promoted instead of contraception, the estimated rate of abortion was 54 per 1,000 women compared to 12 per 1,000 women in western Europe.

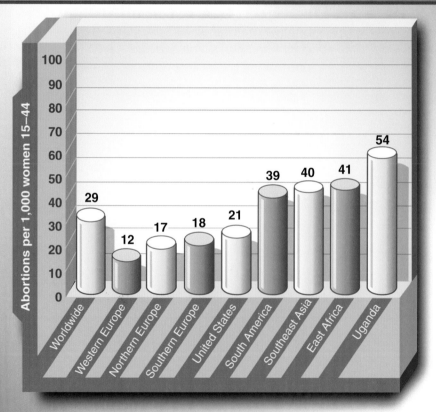

Source: World Health Organization and the Guttmacher Institute, 2007.

- According to the Guttmacher Institute:
  - Publicly supported family planning services prevent **1.3 million** unplanned pregnancies every year. If these pregnancies were to occur, they would result in **832,000** abortions, and increase the U.S. abortion rate by **40 percent**.
  - Publicly funded family planning clinics have helped women prevent **20 million** unintended pregnancies since 1986. An estimated **9 million** of these pregnancies would have ended in abortion.
  - In 2003, the abortion rate for the United States was 20.8 abortions for every 1,000 live births. At the current rate, about **33 percent** of all American women will have had at least one abortion by the time they are 45 years old.
  - Eleven percent of all sexually active women not using contraception account for **46 percent** of all abortions.
  - **Twenty-four** percent of all pregnancies end in abortion.

Key People and Advocacy Groups

Spring Adams: Thirteen-year-old Idaho girl who in 1989 became pregnant after her father raped her. On the morning she was supposed to have an abortion, he shot and killed her. Adams's case is cited by those who oppose efforts to make pregnant minors get parental permission to have an abortion.

Becky Bell: An Indiana teenager who died in 1988 from an illegal abortion. She sought an abortion illegally because she was too ashamed to comply with Indiana's requirement that she notify her parents before being allowed to get an abortion. Her case is cited by those who oppose efforts to make pregnant minors get parental permission to have an abortion.

Rosa DeLauro: Democratic congresswoman from Connecticut who cosponsored the Reducing the Need for Abortion and Supporting Parents Act with Tim Ryan.

Ann Furedi: Chief executive of British Pregnancy Advisory Service (BPAS), the United Kingdom's largest independent abortion provider, and an outspoken advocate for legal access to abortion.

Guttmacher Institute: Research institute for reproductive health and rights. Produces numerous studies and statistics on abortion demographics that are deemed authoritative by both the pro-choice and pro-life camps.

Nancy Keenan: President of NARAL Pro-Choice America, an organization that supports a woman's right to end an unwanted pregnancy.

Norma McCorvey: Known better to the world as "Jane Roe," McCorvey's unwanted pregnancy was used to challenge state laws against abortion.

Because the case lasted so long, McCorvey never actually had an abortion. But her case convinced the Supreme Court to strike down existing state laws against abortion, in effect legalizing it nationwide. Years after the decision, McCorvey said she deeply regretted her role in abortion history and became a devout activist for the right-to-life movement.

National Right to Life: One of the largest antiabortion organizations in the United States. The committee opposes all forms of abortion at all time periods on the grounds that abortion is murder. It encourages the adoption of laws that grant embryos and fetuses the same right to life as born persons.

Planned Parenthood: A national organization that supports women's right to make their own reproductive decisions without governmental interference. It provides contraception, abortion, and family planning services at clinics located throughout the United States. Planned Parenthood clinics are sometimes violently attacked by those who disagree with the services they provide.

Jane Roe: The name given to Norma McCorvey during the landmark Supreme Court case *Roe v. Wade* to protect her privacy.

Tim Ryan: Democratic congressman from Ohio who cosponsored the Reducing the Need for Abortion and Supporting Parents Act with Rosa DeLauro.

Bart Slepian: Abortion doctor who was killed by antiabortionists in 1998.

Amillia Taylor: At 21 weeks and 6 days gestation, Taylor is the youngest baby to ever survive an early birth. Though the odds of survival are very slim at that age, supporters of abortion use Taylor's case to argue that fetuses earlier than 22 weeks should not be able to be aborted if they have even the slightest chance of surviving outside their mother.

Roussel Uclaf: The French pharmaceutical company that developed RU-486, or the abortion pill, in the early 1980s.

Chronology

1821
Connecticut passes the first law in the United States banning abortions after "quickening," or when a woman first feels her baby kick.

1916
Margaret Sanger is jailed after opening the first birth control clinic in the United States.

1960
The U.S. Food and Drug Administration approves the use of oral contraceptives.

1979
In *Belotti v. Baird*, the Supreme Court strikes down a Massachusetts law requiring parental consent for abortions sought by minors. Minors are allowed to obtain permission from a judge instead of a parent.

1973
Abortion is legalized nationwide by the U.S. Supreme Court's decision in *Roe v. Wade*.

1820   1920   1960   1970   1980

1873
Congress passes the Comstock Act, which declares information about contraceptives to be "obscene material."

1962
An increase in babies born deformed as a result of the drug thalidomide taken by their mothers, and from an outbreak of rubella, prompts officials to reexamine laws banning abortion.

1970
Congress enacts Title X of the Public Health Service Act, providing family planning services, education, and research.

Hawaii becomes the first state to repeal criminal abortion laws.

1976
Congress adopts the first Hyde Amendment, which bans the use of federal Medicaid funds to provide abortions to poor women.

1977
The Hyde Amendment is revised to allow states to deny Medicaid funding for abortions except in cases of rape, incest, or threats to the woman's health.

First reported arson at an abortion clinic, in St. Paul, Minnesota, and first known bombing of an abortion clinic, in Cincinnati, Ohio.

1993

Abortion doctor David Gunn is murdered outside of Pensacola Women's Medical Services in Florida.

President Bill Clinton lifts a ban known as the "gag rule," which forbids federally funded clinics from mentioning abortion to their patients.

1997

Two bombs blast outside an Atlanta building containing an abortion clinic; six people are injured; the clinic is left in ruins; and the blast blows out windows across the street.

2007

The U.S. Supreme Court upholds the Partial Birth Abortion Ban Act of 2003 in the cases *Gonzales v. Planned Parenthood* and *Gonzales v. Carhart*. The ban criminalizes abortions done via dilation and extraction in the second trimester of pregnancy, which account for about 0.17 percent of all abortions.

2000

The U.S. Food and Drug Administration approves RU-486, or the "abortion pill," for prescription use.

1990

2000

2007

1994

Dr. John Britton, Lt. Col. Jim Barrett, Shannon Lowney, and Leanne Nichols are murdered in shootings at three abortion clinics.

1995

Norma McCorvey, "Jane Roe" of *Roe v. Wade*, joins the antiabortion group Operation Rescue, declares she is pro-life, and says she regrets her role in the landmark case.

2003

President George W. Bush signs the Partial Birth Abortion Ban Act of 2003, which bans a late-term abortion procedure medically known as dilation and extraction. It is challenged on the grounds it does not contain an exception for the life or health of the mother.

2006

South Dakota governor Mike Rounds signs legislation that makes nearly all abortion procedures illegal in the state and is the harshest antiabortion legislation to be proposed since *Roe v. Wade*. It is eventually overturned.

1992

In the case *Planned Parenthood v. Casey*, the Supreme Court reaffirms the decision of *Roe v. Wade* that women have a right to abortion before fetal viability, but allows states to restrict abortion access so long as these restrictions do not impose an "undue burden" on women seeking abortions. Dozens of states pass laws requiring parental consent or notification for minors' abortions and/or mandatory waiting periods and counseling.

Related Organizations

ACLU Reproductive Freedom Project

125 Broad St. 18th Fl.

New York, NY 10004-2400

(212) 549-2500 • fax: (212) 549-2652

Web site: www.aclu.org/reproductiverights

This is a branch of the American Civil Liberties Union that works to guarantee the constitutional right to reproductive choice. The project produces fact sheets, pamphlets, articles, and reports and publishes the quarterly newsletter *Reproductive Rights Update.*

American Life League (ALL)

PO Box 1350

Stafford, VA 22555

(540) 659-4171 • fax: (540) 659-2586

Web site: www.all.org

The American Life League (ALL) opposes abortion and promotes family values. It disseminates educational materials, books, flyers, and programs for pro-family organizations that oppose abortion. Publications include the biweekly newsletter *Communiqué*, the bimonthly magazine *Celebrate Life*, and the weekly newsletter *Lifefax.*

Americans United for Life (AUL)

310 S. Peoria St., Suite 300

Chicago, IL 60604-3534

(312) 492-7234 • fax: (312) 492-7235

e-mail: information@unitedforlife.org • Web site: www.unitedforlife.org

AUL uses education, litigation, and legislation to pursue efforts to make abortion illegal. The organization operates a library and a legal-resource center. It publishes the quarterly newsletter *Lex Vitae*, the monthly newsletters *AUL Insights* and *AUL Forum*, and numerous booklets.

Catholics for a Free Choice (CFFC)

1436 U St. NW, Suite 301

Washington, DC 20009

(202) 986-6093 • fax: (202) 332-7995

e-mail: cffc@catholicsforchoice.org • Web site: www.cath4choice.org

This organization supports the right of women to access abortion services from a Catholic perspective. CFFC promotes family planning to reduce the need for abortion and to increase women's choice in childbearing and child rearing. It publishes the bimonthly newsletter *Conscience.*

Guttmacher Institute

125 Maiden Ln., 7th Fl.

New York, NY 10038

(212) 248-1111 • fax: (212) 248-1951

e-mail: info@guttmacher.org • Web site: www.guttmacher.org

The institute is a reproduction research group that advocates the right to safe and legal abortion. It provides extensive statistical information on abortion and voluntary population control considered authoritative by both antiabortion and abortion rights groups. Publications include the bimonthly journal *Family Planning Perspectives* and *State Policies in Brief,* helpful compilations of varying state laws on abortion.

National Abortion and Reproductive Rights Action League (NARAL)

1156 15th St. NW, Suite 700

Washington, DC 20005

(202) 973-3000 • fax: (202) 973-3096

e-mail: comments@naral.org • Web site: www.prochoiceamerica.org

NARAL is the nation's leading advocate for privacy and a woman's right to choose. NARAL Pro-Choice America works to protect the pro-choice values of freedom and privacy. It publishes numerous articles, pamphlets, reports, and news briefs about the state of abortion rights in America.

National Conference of Catholic Bishops (NCCB)

3211 Fourth St. NE

Washington, DC 20017-1194

(202) 541-3000 • fax: (202) 541-3322

Web site: www.nccbuscc.org

The NCCB is the American Roman Catholic bishops' organ for unified action. Through its committee on pro-life activities, it advocates a legislative ban on abortion and promotes state restrictions on abortion, such as parental consent/notification laws and strict licensing laws for abortion clinics.

National Right to Life Committee (NRLC)

512 10th St. NW

Washington, DC 20004

(202) 626-8800

e-mail: nrlc@nrlc.org • Web site: www.nrlc.org

NRLC is one of the largest antiabortion organizations in the United States. The committee encourages laws that grant embryos and fetuses the same right to life as born persons and advocates alternatives to abortion, such as adoption. NRLC publishes the brochure *When Does Life Begin?* and the periodic tabloid *National Right to Life News.*

Planned Parenthood Federation of America (PPFA)

810 Seventh Ave.

New York, NY 10019

(212) 541-7800 • fax: (212) 245-1845

e-mail: communications@ppfa.org

Web site: www.plannedparenthood.org

Planned Parenthood is a national organization that supports women's right to make their own reproductive decisions without governmental interference. It provides contraception, abortion, and family planning services at clinics located throughout the United States. Among its extensive publications are the pamphlets *Abortions: Questions and Answers, Five Ways to Prevent Abortion*, and *Nine Reasons Why Abortions Are Legal.*

Pro-Life Action League

6160 N. Cicero Ave., Suite 600

Chicago, IL 60646

(312) 777-2900 • fax: (312) 777-3061

e-mail: scheidler@attglobal.net • Web site: www.prolifeaction.org

The Pro-Life Action League favors the creation of a constitutional amendment that would ban abortion. It conducts demonstrations against abortion clinics and other agencies involved with abortion.

Religious Coalition for Reproductive Choice (RCRC)

1025 Vermont Ave. NW, Suite 1130

Washington, DC 20005

(202) 628-7700 • fax: (202) 628-7716

e-mail: info@rcrc.org • Web site: www.rcrc.org

RCRC is composed of more than 30 Christian, Jewish, and other religious groups committed to enabling individuals to make decisions concerning abortion in accordance with their conscience. The organization supports abortion rights, opposes antiabortion violence, and educates policy makers and the public about the diversity of religious perspectives on abortion.

For Further Research

Books

Erika Bachiochi, ed., *The Cost of Choice: Women Evaluate the Impact of Abortion.* New York: Encounter, 2004.

Francis J. Beckwith, *Defending Life: A Moral and Legal Case Against Abortion Choice.* Cambridge: Cambridge University Press, 2007.

Emma Carlson Berne, ed., *Introducing Issues with Opposing Viewpoints: Abortion.* Detroit, MI: Greenhaven Press, 2007.

Angela Bonavoglia, ed., *The Choices We Made: Twenty-five Women and Men Speak Out About Abortion.* Berkeley, CA: Seal, 2001.

J. Shoshanna Ehrlich, *Who Decides? The Abortion Rights of Teens.* Westport, CT: Praeger, 2006.

Aníbal Faúndes and José S. Barzelatto, *The Human Drama of Abortion: A Global Search for Consensus.* Nashville: Vanderbilt University Press, 2006.

Krista Jacob, ed., *Abortion Under Attack: Women on the Challenges Facing Choice.* Berkeley, CA: Seal, 2006.

Robert Jütte and V. Russell, *Contraception: A History.* Cambridge: Polity, 2008.

Melody Rose, *Safe, Legal, and Unavailable? Abortion Politics in the United States.* Washington, DC: CQ Press, 2006.

Ian Shapiro, ed., *Abortion: The Supreme Court Decisions, 1965–2007.* Indianapolis: Hackett, 2008.

Susan Wicklund and Alan Kesselheim, *This Common Secret: My Journey as an Abortion Doctor.* New York: PublicAffairs, 2007.

Periodicals

Daniela Altimari, "Should Parents Be Notified?" *Hartford (CT) Courant*, March 16, 2007.

Fred Barnes, "Choosing Life: How Pro-lifers Become Pro-lifers," *Weekly Standard*, September 1, 2006.

Catholics for a Free Choice, "Respecting Women's Rights and Fetal Value: Reflections on the Question of Fetal Anesthesia," *Conscience*, Autumn 2005.

Kira Cochrane, "'Abortion on Demand' Is a Myth," *New Statesman*, April 23, 2007.

Susan A. Cohen, "Repeat Abortion, Repeat Unintended Pregnancy, Repeated and Misguided Government Policies," *Guttmacher Policy Review*, vol. 10, no. 2, Spring 2007.

Susan A. Cohen, "Toward Making Abortion 'Rare': The Shifting Battleground over the Means to an End," *Guttmacher Policy Review*, vol. 9, no. 1, Winter 2006.

James D. Davidson, "What Catholics Believe About Abortion and the Death Penalty," *National Catholic Reporter*, September 30, 2005.

Ann Furedi, "Some Messages Can't Be Massaged," *Conscience*, Winter 2006–2007.

Nancy Gibbs, "One Woman at a Time," *Time*, February 26, 2007.

Stan Guthrie, "Don't Cede the High Ground," *Christianity Today*, May 2007.

Patricia Headley, "Parental Notification Is Just Common Sense," *Champaign (IL) News Gazette*, October 4, 2006.

Adele Horin, "The Abortion Pill Is About Women, Not Politics," *Sydney Morning Herald* (Australia), November 12, 2005.

Whitney Hoyt, "Abortion Ruling Trumps State Law," *Marin (CA) Independent Journal*, May 22, 2007.

Ziba Kashef, "Her Body, Her Choice?" *Colorlines*, Winter 2005.

Nina Kohl, "Making Abortion Rare," *Tikkun*, March/April, 2007.

LeeChe Leong, "Virulent Virginity; 'Abstinence-Only' Sex Ed Programs Are Putting Youth at Risk," *Colorlines*, vol. 7, no. 4, January 31, 2005.

John R. Lott, "Abortion and Crime: One Has an Effect on the Other, but It May Not Be the Effect You Think," *National Review*, August 13, 2007.

John F. McManus, "Abortion's Effect on America," *New American*, January 23, 2006.

Caitlin Moran, "Abortion: Why It's the Ultimate Motherly Act," *Times* (London), April 13, 2007. http://timesonline.co.uk.

National Review, "Partial Truth About Partial-Birth," May 14, 2007.

National Right to Life News, "The Missing: The Real Impact of Abortion on American Society," January 2007.

Sarah Nelson, "The Partial Birth Abortion Ban—Effects on Women's Rights, Up Close & Personal," *Women's Health Activist*, July/August 2007.

Susan Nielsen, "Abortion Law Hits Home for Happy Families, Too," Portland *Oregonian*, October 29, 2006.

Drea Olmstead, "Secrecy Not the Answer in Abortion Decision," Eugene (OR) *Register-Guard*, November 3, 2006.

Bill O'Reilly, "Secular Progressives Keep Parents in the Dark," *Columbia (MO) Daily Tribune*, October 28, 2006.

Ramesh Ponnuru, "Winning, and Losing, on Abortion: How Go the Wars?" *National Review*, May 8, 2006.

Anna Quindlen, "The Clinic: A No-Spin Zone," *Newsweek*, October 16, 2006.

Cindy Richards, "Notification: It's Time to Use Good Sense," *Chicago Sun-Times*, January 24, 2007.

Amanda Robb, "Last Clinic Standing," *Marie Claire*, October 2006.

Rosemary Radford Ruether, "'Consistent Life Ethic' Is Inconsistent," *National Catholic Reporter*, November 17, 2006.

Scott Schaeffer-Duff, "Christians Must Reject All Killing," *National Catholic Reporter*, February 23, 2007.

Elizabeth Schulte, "Is the Past a Prologue for the Roberts-Alito Court? Abortion Before *Roe*," Counterpunch.org, January 20, 2006. www.counterpunch.org.

Ann V. Shibler, "Saving Babies, One at a Time," *New American*, August 20, 2007.

Gretchen Voss, "The Easiest Choice I Ever Made," *Marie Claire*, March 2007.

Ayelete Waldman, "Looking Abortion in the Face," *Salon.com*, February 9, 2005. http://dir.salon.com.

Judith Warner, "When the Parents Can't Know," *New York Times*, July 29, 2006.

Web Sites

Abortion Concern (www.abortionconcern.org)

Abortion Is Pro-Life (www.abortionisprolife.com)

Feminist Women's Health Center page on Abortion (www.fwhc.org)

Medical Abortion Information (www.medicationabortion.com)

Men and Abortion (www.menandabortion.com)

National Abortion Federation (NAF) (www.prochoice.org)

Post Abortion Healing Help (http://afterabortion.com)

Source Notes

Overview

1. Kira Cochrane, "'Abortion on Demand' Is a Myth," *New Statesman*, April 23, 2007, p. 22.
2. Gretchen Voss, "The Easiest Choice I Ever Made Is Also the Hardest to Live With," *Marie Claire*, March 2007, p. 131.
3. Patricia E. Bauer, "The Abortion Debate No One Wants to Have," *Washington Post*, October 18, 2005, p. A25.
4. Ayelet Waldman, "Looking Abortion in the Face," *Salon.com*, February 9, 2005. http://dir.salon.com.
5. Quoted in Laura Echevarria, "Not an 'Error' but Our Child," National Right to Life, July 31, 2006. www.nrlc.org.
6. Douglas A. Sylva, "The Lost Girls: Sex-Selective Abortions Are Targeting Unborn Girls by the Millions," *Weekly Standard*, March 15, 2007.
7. Sylva, "Lost Girls," p. ?.
8. "State Facts About Abortion: South Dakota," Guttmacher Institute, 2006. www.guttmacher.org.
9. Diana Dukhanova, "The Junk Science of Abortion-Breast Cancer Syndrome," *Tikkun*, vol. 21, no. 1, April 2001, p. 26.
10. "The Transformative Power of Post-Abortion Syndrome," *National Right to Life News*, March 2007, p. 2.
11. Quoted in Cynthia L. Cooper, "Abortion Under Attack," *Ms.*, August, 2001.

Is Abortion Moral?

12. "Interview: *Canticle* talks with Miss Norma McCorvey," *Canticle*, no. 8, Winter 2000.
13. Anonymous, "A Personal Perspective," *National Right to Life News*, February 2006, p. 3.
14. Rosemary Radford Ruether, "'Consistent Life Ethic' Is Inconsistent," *National Catholic Reporter*, November 17, 2006, p. 13.
15. Voss, "The Easiest Choice I Ever Made," p. 131.
16. Ruether, "'Consistent Life Ethic' Is Inconsistent," p. 14.
17. Waldman, "Looking Abortion in the Face."
18. *National Review*, "Some People Try to Split the Difference on Abortion by Saying that the Unborn Should Be Protected After 'Viability' but Not Before It," March 19, 2007, p. 6.
19. Quoted in Nancy Gibbs, "1 Woman at a Time," *Time*, February 26, 2007, p. 22.
20. Quoted in Ziba Kashef, "Her Body, Her Choice?" *Colorlines*, Winter 2005, p. 42.
21. Caitlin Moran, "Abortion: Why It's the Ultimate Motherly Act," *Times* (London), April 13, 2007. http://timesonline.co.uk.
22. Ruether, "'Consistent Life Ethic' Is Inconsistent," p. 13.
23. Hanes Swingle, "A Doctor's Grisly Experience with Abortion," *Washington Times*, July 23, 2003.
24. Susan J. Lee et al., "Fetal Pain: A Systematic Multidisciplinary Review of the Evidence," *Journal of the American Medical Association*, vol. 294, no. 8, August 24–31, 2005, p. 952. http://jama.ama-assn.org.
25. Catholics for a Free Choice, "Respecting Women's Rights and Fetal Value: Reflections on the Question of Fetal

Anesthesia," *Conscience*, Autumn 2005, p. 39.

26. Swingle, "A Doctor's Grisly Experience with Abortion."

Should Abortion Be Legal?

27. *Roe v. Wade* (No. 70-18), 314 F.Supp. 1217, affirmed in part and reversed in part. www.law.cornell.edu.

28. *Roe v. Wade* (No. 70-18), 314 F. Supp. 1217.

29. Roe v. Wade (No. 70-18), 314 F. Supp. 1217.

30. President Bush Signs Unborn Victims of Violence Act of 2004, April 1, 2004. www.whitehouse.gov.

31. Quoted in Douglas Johnson, "Seeing 1 When There are 2," *National Review*, February 5, 2004.

32. Steven D. Levitt and Stephen J. Dubner, *Freakonomics*. New York: Harper-Collins, 2005, p. 139.

33. Quoted in Kate Zernike, "30 Years After *Roe v. Wade*, New Trends but the Old Debate," *New York Times*, January 30, 2003.

34. Nina Kohl, "Making Abortion Rare," *Tikkun*, March/April, 2007, p. 40.

35. Cochrane, "'Abortion on Demand' Is a Myth," p. 21.

36. Susan A. Cohen, "Repeat Abortion, Repeat Unintended Pregnancy, Repeated and Misguided Government Policies," *Guttmacher Policy Review*, vol. 10, no. 2, Spring 2007.

37. Faye Wattleton, interviewed in Akiba Solomon, "The Battle for Reproductive Rights," *Essence*, May 2006, p. 136.

38. Wattleton, "The Battle for Reproductive Rights," p. 136.

39. Susan A. Cohen, "Toward Making Abortion 'Rare': The Shifting Battleground over the Means to an End," *Guttmacher Policy Review*, vol. 9, no. 1, Winter 2006.

40. Quoted in Anna Quindlen, "The Clinic: A No-Spin Zone," *Newsweek*, October 16, 2006, p. 82.

What Restrictions Should Be Placed on Abortion?

41. Boston Women's Health Book Collective, *Our Bodies Ourselves for the New Century*. New York: Touchstone, 1998, p. 412.

42. Quoted in Daniela Altimari, "Should Parents Be Notified?" *Hartford (CT) Courant*, March 16, 2007, p. B2.

43. Patricia Headley, "Parental Notification Is Just Common Sense," Champaign (IL) *News Gazette*, October 4, 2006, p. A8.

44. Drea Olmstead, "Secrecy Not the Answer in Abortion Decision," Eugene, (OR) *Register-Guard*, November 3, 2006, p. A13.

45. Susan Nielsen, "Abortion Law Hits Home for Happy Families, Too," *Portland Oregonian*, October 29, 2006, p. F1.

46. Richard Pan, "No on Prop 73: Measure Could Put Teens at Risk," *Sacramento (CA) Bee*, October 15, 2005, p. B17.

47. Susan Nielsen, "Abortion Law Hits Home for Happy Families, Too," *Oregonian (Portland, OR)*, October 29, 2006, p. F1.

48. Quoted in "World's Youngest Baby Born in Miami: Amillia Taylor Born After 21 Weeks, 6 days," Local 10 News, February 19, 2007. www.local10.com.

49. *National Review*, "Partial Truth About Partial-Birth," May 14, 2007, p. 14.

50. Quoted in "U.S. Supreme Court Rules Federal Abortion Ban Constitutional," SIECUS Policy Updates, April 2007. www.siecus.org.

51. Quoted in Linda Greenhouse, "Justices Back Ban on Method of Abor-

tion," *New York Times*, April 19, 2007. www.nytimes.com.

What Measures Might Reduce the Need for Abortion?

52. NorineDworkin-McDaniel,"Betrayed by a Pill," *Marie Claire*, July 2007, p. 184.

53. Quoted in *Human Events*, "Capital Briefs," October 6, 2000.

54. Terri Foran, "Debating the 'Abortion Pill,'" *Australian Doctor*, December 2, 2005, p. 33.

55. Dworkin-McDaniel, "Betrayed by a Pill," p. 186.

56. Cynthia Dailard, "Promoting Prevention to Reduce the Need for Abortion: Good Policy, Good Politics," *Guttmacher Report on Public Policy*, vol. 8, no. 2, May 2005.

57. Kathy Clay-Little, "In the Real World, the Facts About Sex Are Necessary," *San Antonio (TX) Express-News*, October 8, 2007, p. 7B.

58. Cohen, "Toward Making Abortion 'Rare.'"

59. Jessica Mac, "Making the Best Decision for My Son," The Cradle.com. Accessed December 18, 2007.

List of Illustrations

Index

About the Author

Lauri S. Friedman earned her bachelor's degree in religion and political science from Vassar College in 1999. Her studies there focused on political Islam, and she produced a thesis on the Islamic Revolution in Iran titled *Neither West, Nor East, but Islam.* She also holds a preparatory degree in flute performance from the Manhattan School of Music.

She is the founder of LSF Editorial, a writing and editing outfit in San Diego. Her clients include ReferencePoint Press, for whom she has written *The Death Penalty, Nuclear Weapons and Security*, and *Terrorist Attacks*, all in the Compact Research series.

Friedman lives in Ocean Beach, San Diego, with her fiancé, Randy, and their yellow lab, Trucker. In her spare time she enjoys pottery, making music, and traveling.